GOLF · A WAY OF LIFE GOLF · A WAY OF LIFE GOLF · A WAY OF LIFE GOLF · A WAY OF LIFE
GOLF · A WAY OF LIFE GOLF · A WAY OF LIFE GOLF · A WAY OF LIFE GOLF · A WAY OF LIFE
GOLF · A WAY OF LIFE GOLF · A WAY OF LIFE GOLF · A WAY OF LIFE GOLF · A WAY OF LIFE
GOLF · A WAY OF LIFE GOLF · A WAY OF LIFE GOLF · A WAY OF LIFE GOLF · A WAY OF LIFE
GOLF · A WAY OF LIFE GOLF · A WAY OF LIFE GOLF · A WAY OF LIFE GOLF · A WAY OF LIFE
GOLF · A WAY OF LIFE GOLF · A WAY OF LIFE GOLF · A WAY OF LIFE GOLF · A WAY OF LIFE
GOLF · A WAY OF LIFE GOLF · A WAY OF LIFE GOLF · A WAY OF LIFE GOLF · A WAY OF LIFE
GOLF · A WAY OF LIFE GOLF · A WAY OF LIFE GOLF · A WAY OF LIFE GOLF · A WAY OF LIFE
GOLF · A WAY OF LIFE GOLF · A WAY OF LIFE GOLF · A WAY OF LIFE GOLF · A WAY OF LIFE
GOLF · A WAY OF LIFE GOLF · A WAY OF LIFE GOLF · A WAY OF LIFE GOLF · A WAY OF LIFE
GOLF · A WAY OF LIFE GOLF · A WAY OF LIFE GOLF · A WAY OF LIFE GOLF · A WAY OF LIFE
GOLF · A WAY OF LIFE GOLF · A WAY OF LIFE GOLF · A WAY OF LIFE GOLF · A WAY OF LIFE
GOLF · A WAY OF LIFE GOLF · A WAY OF LIFE GOLF · A WAY OF LIFE GOLF · A WAY OF LIFE
GOLF · A WAY OF LIFE GOLF · A WAY OF LIFE GOLF · A WAY OF LIFE GOLF · A WAY OF LIFE
GOLF · A WAY OF LIFE GOLF · A WAY OF LIFE GOLF · A WAY OF LIFE GOLF · A WAY OF LIFE
GOLF · A WAY OF LIFE GOLF · A WAY OF LIFE GOLF · A WAY OF LIFE GOLF · A WAY OF LIFE
GOLF · A WAY OF LIFE GOLF · A WAY OF LIFE GOLF · A WAY OF LIFE GOLF · A WAY OF LIFE
GOLF · A WAY OF LIFE GOLF · A WAY OF LIFE GOLF · A WAY OF LIFE GOLF · A WAY OF LIFE
GOLF · A WAY OF LIFE GOLF · A WAY OF LIFE GOLF · A WAY OF LIFE GOLF · A WAY OF LIFE
GOLF · A WAY OF LIFE GOLF · A WAY OF LIFE GOLF · A WAY OF LIFE GOLF · A WAY OF LIFE
GOLF · A WAY OF LIFE GOLF · A WAY OF LIFE GOLF · A WAY OF LIFE GOLF · A WAY OF LIFE
GOLF · A WAY OF LIFE GOLF · A WAY OF LIFE GOLF · A WAY OF LIFE GOLF · A WAY OF LIFE
GOLF · A WAY OF LIFE GOLF · A WAY OF LIFE GOLF · A WAY OF LIFE GOLF · A WAY OF LIFE
GOLF · A WAY OF LIFE GOLF · A WAY OF LIFE GOLF · A WAY OF LIFE GOLF · A WAY OF LIFE
GOLF · A WAY OF LIFE GOLF · A WAY OF LIFE GOLF · A WAY OF LIFE GOLF · A WAY OF LIFE

GOLF-A WAY OF LIFE

STANLEY
PAUL

GOLF-A WAY OF LIFE
An Illustrated History of Golf
Edited by Peter Alliss

STANLEY PAUL
London Melbourne Auckland Johannesburg

THE CONTRIBUTORS
Keith Mackie, formerly editor of *Golf World*
John Campbell, golf contributor to the *Daily Telegraph*
John Hopkins, golf correspondent of the *Sunday Times*
Michael Williams, golf correspondent of the *Daily Telegraph*
David Davies, golf correspondent of *The Guardian*

Stanley Paul & Co. Ltd

An imprint of Century Hutchinson Ltd
62-65 Chandos Place, London WC2N 4NW
Century Hutchinson (Australia) Pty Ltd
16-22 Church Street, Hawthorn, Melbourne, Victoria 3122
Century Hutchinson (NZ) Ltd
191 Archers Road, Glenfield, Auckland 10
Century Hutchinson (SA) Pty Ltd
PO Box 337 Bergvlei 2012, South Africa

First published 1987
Copyright © Lennard Books 1987

Made by Lennard Books Ltd
Mackerye End, Harpenden, Herts AL5 5DR

Editor Michael Leitch
Designed by Pocknell & Co
Editorial Consultant Chris Plumridge

British Library Cataloguing in Publication Data
Golf: a way of life
1. Golf
I. Alliss, Peter
796.352 GV965

ISBN 0 09 166510 8

Printed and bound in Great Britain
by Butler & Tanner Ltd, Frome and London

Jacket Photographs

Front
Top left Jack Nicklaus.
Top centre Harry Vardon.
Top right Billy Casper.

Back
Left Jan Stephenson.
Centre Dai Rees.
Right Seve Ballesteros.

CONTENTS

I was born into golf, indeed the Alliss family has been associated with the game since before the First World War. My father, Percy Alliss, came from Sheffield. He was one of a large family which ran a smallholding near the site of the present Hallam Towers Hotel. As a lad he used to earn a bit of extra pocket money caddying at the Hallamshire Golf Club.

By the time I came along, Father was an established golf professional with many national titles under his belt, and golf was our life. In 1932 the family moved back to England from Berlin, where my father had been senior professional at the Wannsee Golf-und-Land Club, and after a couple of years at Beaconsfield and Temple Newsam Golf Clubs we settled at Ferndown GC in Dorset. That was where I spent my growing-up years, in the glorious heather-and-pine country surrounding the golf course, with occasional excursions into Bournemouth.

In 1946 I went up to Edinburgh to take part in the Boys' Championship and shortly afterwards, at the age of fifteen, I left school and became a golf professional, working as assistant (unpaid) to my father. My future in golf seemed assured, and that is how it has turned out, though not remotely in ways I could have predicted at the time.

As I look back on it all, I think how lucky I have been that things were as they were in those distant days just after the war. Changes there have been, of course, and many, but the 1940s and '50s gave me my start in golf and the chance to make my livelihood from the game.

A year or two ago I remember Neil Kinnock, the Labour leader, telling an audience that his involvement with his Party had provided him with virtually everything he had in life – an education, the chance to meet and discuss things with people more knowledgeable and experienced than himself, the chance to travel the world and to build up a special kind of friendship and camaraderie that is not afforded to many. I consider that golf has done very much the same for me.

To a young man starting out when I did, the idea that you could actually make a living solely from playing golf was – unless you were Henry Cotton – an ideological dream. If you played well enough to compete in the eight or nine tournaments available each year, that was a bonus. Your real life, however, was centred on a golf club, and when your tournament-playing days were over you went back to the club full-time and spent your days giving lessons and quietly working out your time in one of the most beautiful natural settings in your part of the country.

People today are surprised by this description of the pro golfer's life. They say to me, 'Ah, but you must have had other ambitions. You must have felt some inner urge to become the greatest golfer the world has ever seen.'

Not true. In those days it was not fashionable to travel far, especially not to somewhere as distant as the United States. It was enough of a slog to get round Britain on those pre-motorway roads – up to St Andrews, down to Leeds and then over to Llandudno or Sandwich, and always back to the club, back to your prime duty in life, which was to keep the members happy. From our country backwaters we marvelled at people like Bobby Locke and the young Gary Player for daring to risk their careers by going to play in far-off lands, and we found their success quite staggering.

It is fair to say, too, that the incentives to travel and take such risks were not what they are today. Prize-money was small and expenses were relatively high. A lot of us were happy to settle for being a medium-sized fish in a small pond. It wasn't a bad life, either. In fact, it was a good life. After all, to be considered one of the best golf players in a country with a population of around fifty million was no small thing.

Perhaps it was rather unambitious thinking. It was, though, typical of the way the British tournament professional looked upon his career and prospects through the Fifties and into the Sixties. Compare that with the brisk young men of the Eighties who can't wait to get out there and chance their arm on the now lucrative European Tour, and you can see that a lot of fundamental changes have taken place in, historically, a very short time.

In this book you will find a series of forty-three chapters, written by five wise and eminent golf journalists of our day, which investigate the history and character of the game of golf. And what an extraordinary, unique game it is. To some it is pedestrian and slow; to others it is the complete game, one which calls for stamina and mental toughness allied to physical skills and control which are second to none in the worlds of sport and recreation.

Take just some of the game's extraordinary aspects. The stationary ball. The side-on approach. The absence of sharing a ball plus the isolation of the player. The absence of physical contact (which in our super-competitive times has certainly damaged a few other games). The natural terrain. The memorable pleasures of a perfectly hit shot. The successful reading of a difficult green. The fact that every golf course is different (you can't say that about tennis courts or football stadiums).

In the last hundred years the game has grown and spread to all corners of the world – to the arid deserts of West Texas, to Mexico City and Johannesburg, to the islands of the Pacific, to the shadows of Mount Fuji. And yet, despite all this growth and expansion, the basics of golf have changed very little. The game is still played sideways-on; the shape of the clubs is generally the same, even though their performance, and that of the all-important ball, has been considerably improved; the dimensions of the hole are the same, although many have thought of making it larger (thank goodness they have not!).

It would be foolhardy, nonetheless, to claim that golf has not moved with the times. Think of the way the courses have been transformed. Those velvet swards we stride about today bear scant comparison to the greens of yesteryear, which the head greenkeeper used to cut with a scythe. His blade, mark you, was as sharp as a hussar's sword; even so, no matter how many times the head man swished it over the putting surface, to and fro until the grass was satisfactorily shaved, the end result could only have been, to our eyes, relatively even.

Strange, then, that in an age where the lush and watered pastures of Augusta seem to many to represent golfing perfection, the greatest mecca of all is St Andrews, and the greatest prize for the golfing pilgrim is to play one round on the Old Course. A course which, if you designed and built such a thing today, you would run a considerable risk of not being paid. 'Call that a golf course?' they would say. 'It's just a piece of bumpy old linksland. You haven't done any work! And double greens? How can you have double greens? Are you out of your mind? And crossover fairways?'

The wrath and incomprehension of your clients would be boundless. And yet, of course, it all works, and works quite brilliantly, bringing doom and frustration – and corresponding bursts of the purest joy – to generation after generation of golfers at every level of the game. Bobby Jones tore up his card there on his first visit, saying it was just too difficult and silly; but he could not rest until he had returned and conquered it, as he did in the 1927 Open. Many since have understood how he felt, even if they were unable to emulate him.

This tremendous scope for variation within the game, polarized by the very different challenges of Augusta and St Andrews, must be one of its greatest strengths. In between, what is there? Why, a thousand beautiful places. What could be better than Wentworth, or Banff Springs in autumn? Or Pebble Beach in California? A day in good company at Turnberry or Royal St George's? Or far to the north at Nairn or Royal Dornoch? Or down to one of those gems in the West Country: St Mellion, Trevose or Saunton?

I could go on. Suffice to say, if you got your timing right you could spend a lifetime searching for your favourite golf course. Now there's a project I would warmly recommend.

PART ONE

THE EARLY YEARS

Golf was not invented – it was born out of boredom. As man's ability to think began to outstrip the mundane necessities of survival he looked for ways of filling his time with more pleasurable pursuits. Every civilization throughout history has moved in roughly the same direction – developing the ability to throw a stone into the desire to hit it with a stick.

The Chinese certainly played a stick-and-ball game; the Japanese are making a belated claim to have fathered golf – a paternity suit which will be hotly contested!; engravings in the tombs of the Pharaohs show protagonists with implements like hockey sticks; in Greek and Roman times ball games were very popular, and so the progress goes on through Germany, France, Belgium and the Netherlands.

The exact form these games took is impossible to determine because early historical records usually show no more than a vague illustration of a man with a stick hitting something or someone. Trying to trace a strict line of descent for golf through this labyrinth is impossible. The massive variety of games played with a stick and a ball today highlight the problem. Accepting a wide variation in the shape and form of the 'sticks' and 'balls', you can bracket together such diverse pastimes as croquet and cricket. While there is evidence of closer blood-ties between hockey and shinty, tennis and badminton, there is no obvious connection between golf and ice-hockey other than the fact that they are played with roughly similar implements. Yet if these two games had been illustrated in the crude fashion of five or six hundred years ago – figures outlined in silhouette brandishing their clubs – who would have been able to tell the difference?

What is obvious is that games using sticks and balls were played in many countries over thousands of years. Their exact form is impossible to determine, but it is equally obvious that their forms, styles and rules varied enormously.

Scotland has long been accepted as the home of golf, and despite recent claims from Japan that they actually started the game in the first century, and from the Chinese that their well-known Suigan, which was certainly being played in the early 1300s, was really golf, the only serious contender to Scotland's title comes from the Netherlands.

Evidence does exist of a game with some of the characteristics of golf being played in the village of Loenen as far back as 1296, but details of its form and character are vague, and certainly not strong enough to support the supposition that this was golf in the making.

The earliest illustration of a game which could have had some connection with golf appears in a Flemish Book of Hours dating from 1530, more than seventy years after James II banned the game of golf in Scotland by an Act of Parliament in order to encourage the population to spend more time on archery practice. This was considered more useful in the continuing battles with the English than the ability to get round the local links in a record score.

Most illustrations of the Dutch game, known as *kolven*, show it being played on ice and date from around 1600. It did not apparently last long. Probably it failed through lack of land space, which forced the Dutch to play *kolven* on ice during the winter and on very small areas of dry land in summer. The true game of golf did not appear in Holland until the 1830s.

Scotland's east coast gave birth to golf because of its land formation – large areas of links land which lay between the arable farmland and the sea. Areas which would not support agriculture and would offer useful grazing to no more than a handful of sheep or goats ran right up to the edges of the coastal towns and villages. They became natural places for recreation – and catching rabbits.

Golf, as it is known and played throughout the world today, probably started on just such a stretch of links land by pure chance. Imagine a local lad guarding his father's two sheep as they searched for edible grass among the dunes. After throwing stones at a rabbit hole for some minutes he quickly gets bored and starts swiping at the gorse bushes with a stick,

then he tries hitting a stone with the stick. Weeks, months, even years later he starts to aim at the nearest rabbit hole – and so, over years and generations, other people started to carve tree branches to create better clubs, balls were shaped from pieces of wood rather than using stones and it became a simple, logical if lengthy

step to compete against an opponent, trying to hit a ball into a hole in the least number of strokes.

James II's Act of Parliament in 1457 is the earliest recorded reference to golf so far discovered. Much has been made of the fact that a similar Act, passed by the Scottish Parliament under James I in 1424, forbade the playing of football. This Act, however, did not mention golf, the suggestion being that golf was unknown or not popular at the earlier date.

Such an assumption could be very misleading. Just suppose that in 1424 the game of golf was already so popular that no government could readily countenance banning it; but rather took the easy option and outlawed the upstart game of football.

By the later date James II, a clever and ruthless monarch, was determined to drive the English from their two remaining strongholds at Roxburgh and Berwick and was not the sort of man to hesitate over the feelings and opinions of the country's golfers. Unfortunately there is no firm evidence to support either theory – but one is as possible as the other.

Certainly in the early days of golf no-one thought to organize it into clubs, regions or associations or to write about it. From the positive fact that golf was a popular sport in Scotland in 1457 it is also known that no golf clubs were officially formed or records kept for another two hundred years, although the game's

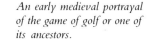

An early medieval portrayal of the game of golf or one of its ancestors.

following grew ever larger during this period.

It will always be impossible to put an exact date on the birth of golf, but it has been played in Scotland without a break for well over five hundred years. All the evidence points to Scotland being the true home of golf. Claims from the Netherlands and further afield are just so much double-Dutch.

Two Scottish golfers caught red-handed while playing their Sunday round. Left A Dutch-style tee shot.

No ordinary club golfer in the world knows and understands every clause, sub-clause, appendix and nuance of the rules of golf. They run to 75 pages, 36 definitions, 41 rules of play and more than 300 sub-sections.

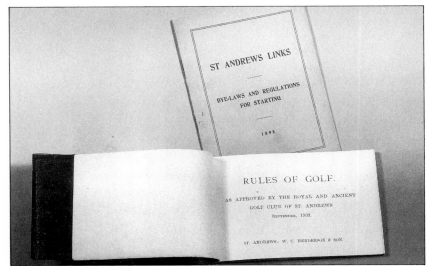

An early copy of The Rules of Golf *printed in St Andrews for the R & A, and the starting regulations for the St Andrews links, many of which are still in force today.*
Right *A description of 'goff' from an early 19th-century edition of Hoyle.*

Because golf is played over open country with no two courses the same and because the golfer and his golf ball can get themselves into such diverse and sometimes ridiculous situations, the rules are necessarily broad, if not cumbersome. They have not always been so.

In those ever more attractive early days of the game the only rules were those agreed and accepted by the players themselves. They differed from one area to another and the game had been played for at least two hundred years, maybe many more, before anyone felt it necessary to commit the basic rules of the game to paper.

The reason for the sudden formality was a request from a group of golfers at Leith –'gentlemen of honour, skillfull in the ancient and healthful exercise of the golf' – to the Magistrates and Council of Edinburgh for a silver golf club to be presented at an annual event over Leith Links. The decision of Edinburgh City Council is recorded in a deliberate hand in the voluminous minutes. The date was 7 March 1744. It was a significant turning point in the game's history, bringing rules and formality to a sport which had enjoyed blissful freedom for centuries. The minutes read:

'It being represented in Council that gentlemen of honour, skillfull in the ancient and healthful exercise of the golf had applied for a silver club to be annually played for on the Links of Leith at such times and upon such conditions as the Magistrates and Council should think proper.

'And it being reported that the Gentlemen Golfers had drawn up a scroll at the desire of the Magistrates, of such articles and conditions as to them seemed most expedient, as proper regulations to be observed by the Gentlemen who should yearly offer to play for the said Silver Club, which were produced and read in Council, the tenor of which follows:

'As many Noblemen or Gentlemen or other Golfers from any part of Great Britain or Ireland as shall book themselves eight days before, or upon any of the lawful days of the week immediately preceeding the day appointed by the Magistrates and Council for the Annual Match, shall have the priviledge of playing for the said Club, each signer paying five shillings Sterling at signing, in a book to be provided for that purpose, which is to ly in Mrs. Clephen's house in Leith, or such other house as afterwards the subscribers shall appoint from year to year; and the regulation approved by the Magistrates and Council shall be recorded at the beginning of said Book.

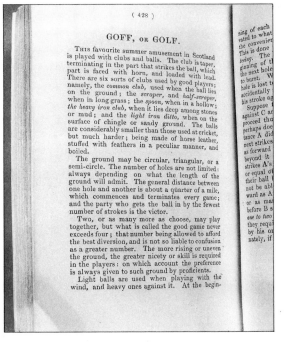

'On the morning before playing, small bits of paper marked with the figures 1, 2, 3, 4 etc according to the number of players shall be put into a bonnet and drawn by the signers and every couple shall be matched according to the figures by them drawn...'

And so on in the greatest of detail. Clerks were to accompany each match and their books and jottings scrutinized at the conclusion, the player winning the greatest number of holes to be declared the winner. If two or more players had won an equal number of holes they were to play another round to decide the outright winner.

Having persuaded the city council to put up a trophy worth £50, not an inconsiderable amount of money in 1744, the Gentlemen Golfers then had to put on paper the regulations governing play. These were the normal rules of play accepted for matches played over Leith Links, but they had never been written down before. They were simple, straight to the point and easily understood by noblemen, gentlemen and even other golfers. Under the heading 'Articles and Laws in playing Golf (The Rules of the Gentlemen Golfers 1744)' they stated:

1. You must tee your ball within a club's length of the hole.
2. Your tee must be on the ground.
3. You are not to change the ball which you strike off the tee.
4. You are not to remove stones, bones or any break club for the sake of playing your ball, except upon the fair green, and that only within a club's length of your ball.
5. If your ball comes among watter, or any wattery filth, you are at liberty to take out your ball and bringing it behind the hazard and teeing it, you may play it with any club and allow your adversary a stroke for so getting out your ball.
6. If your balls be found anywhere touching one another you are to lift the first ball till you play the last.
7. At holling you are to play your ball honestly for the hole, and not to play upon your adversary's ball, not lying in your way to the hole.
8. If you should lose your ball, by its being taken up, or any other way, you are to go back to the spot where you struck last and drop another ball and allow your adversary a stroke for the misfortune.

9. No man at holling his ball is to be allowed to mark his way to the hole with his club or anything else.
10. If a ball be stopp'd by any person, horse, dog, or any thing else, the ball so stopp'd must be played where it lyes.
11. If you draw your club in order to strike and proceed so far in the stroke as to be bringing down your club; if then your club shall break in any way, it is to be accounted a stroke.
12. He whose ball lyes farthest from the hole is obliged to play first.
13. Neither trench, ditch, or dyke made for the preservation of the links, nor the Scholar's Holes or the soldier's lines shall be accounted a hazard but the ball is to be taken out teed and play'd with any iron club.

These first rules of golf were signed by John Rattray, captain of the Gentlemen Golfers, a surgeon who was to serve with Bonnie Prince Charlie's army at the Battle of Prestonpans a year later. Winners of the Silver Club at Leith were obliged to append a gold or silver piece to the club, but, in the quaint wording of the council minutes the five shillings entry fee paid by every competitor was 'solely to be at the disposal of the victor'.

There was one further stipulation: 'Every victor shall, at the receiving of the club, give sufficient caution to the Magistrates and Council for fifty pounds sterling for delivering back the club to their hands one month before it is to be played for again.'

They weren't taking any chances.

An illustration of the game from the Illustrated London Almanack *of 1864.*

T he earliest recorded reference to the purchase of golf equipment appears in the accounts of the Lord High Treasurer of Scotland in an entry dated February 1503. It reads simply: 'Item – to golf clubbes and ballis to the King.' That was James IV. Just over a hundred years later James VI appointed William Mayne, bowyer and burgess of Edinburgh, 'maker of bows, arros, spears and clubs to the

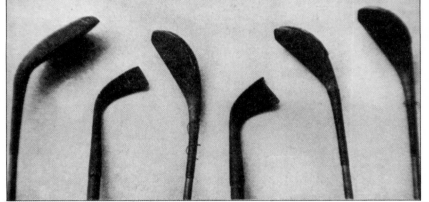

Some of the oldest clubs in existence. These were found at a house in Hull.
Above right A 'guttie' ball sits between two early clubs made by Willie Park and his son; at the back is a rut iron and in the foreground a niblick.

King'. This is the first mention of a specialist club maker.

Surprisingly, there is only a handful of references to clubmakers over the next three hundred and fifty years and then a sudden explosion of them occurred in about 1850. In 1687 Thomas Kincaid described the golf clubs of the day as having shafts of hazel which should be long and supple with the head at a very obtuse angle to the shaft. These elegant clubs, very much collectors' pieces today, had long, narrow, beautifully shaped heads which were fixed to the shafts by a method known as scaring. A V-shaped cut was made deep in the neck of the wooden head and the shaft tapered to be an exact fit. The two were glued together and binding fixed tightly around the entire joint. This was the type of joint used by boatbuilders in making masts and the binding used on golf clubs often consisted of lengths of unravelled rope strands. This binding or whipping survives on modern clubs, where it is largely cosmetic, the new joints being quite strong enough without assistance.

From about 1825 hickory replaced hazel for all club shafts. This American wood was very strong and had wonderfully springy qualities ideally suited to golf.

Until the mid-19th century most golf

clubs were made with wooden heads, usually blackthorn, apple or beech. This was mainly because the 'featherie' balls (see next chapter for details) were so easily split by a slightly mishit iron shot. A typical set would contain perhaps a dozen assorted woods, one iron with a large, lofted face for getting out of bunkers and a very short-headed iron for extracting the ball from difficult lies such as the bottom of a cart rut – hence its name, the rut iron.

The introduction of the gutta-percha ball in 1848 had a dramatic effect on golf-club design. So hard and unyielding was the new ball in comparison to the faithful but expensive featherie that many cherished wooden clubs soon showed terrible signs of wear and tear. Clubfaces were badly dented and cracked and leather inserts were fitted to soften the impact of club with ball.

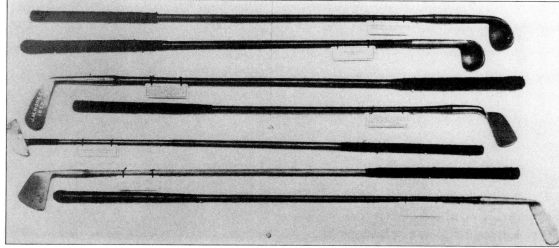

A selection of early clubs from the Wood Collection.

The heavier ball also made control more difficult with the long, slender clubheads and long shafts. Well before the end of the 19th century the shape of wooden clubheads changed completely. From being some 5 in (13 cm) long with the face only 1 in (2.5 cm) deep and the head no wider than 2 in (5 cm), the new breed of clubs were 1 in (2.5 cm) shorter in the head, much broader and had faces almost twice as deep.

In addition, the traditional concave face of the long-headed clubs gave way to exactly the opposite. It was discovered that a slightly convex face had the effect of minimizing both hook and slice spin, and because the centre of their face jutted forward the new clubs became known as 'bulgers'. This new head shape effectively concentrated the weight of the club in a smaller area and led to more consistent and powerful contact with the new ball. At the same time shaft lengths were reduced from 45 to 42 in (1.14 to 1.07 m), giving considerably greater control. The shape of wooden heads has changed remarkably little since.

Between 1885 and 1900 the number of golf clubs and societies in Britain increased by some two thousand as the game experienced a spectacular boom. Imports of hickory shafts increased to more than 100,000 per year and with the discovery that persimmon, another native American wood, had all the perfect qualities for club heads, America was soon exporting completed clubs to Britain.

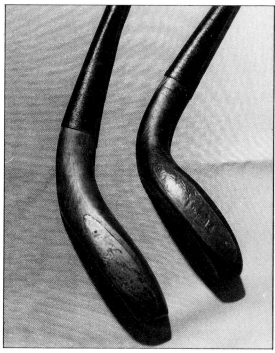

Far left 19th-century woods, strengthened to cope with the new gutta-percha ball.

15

Although mass production took away much of the elegance and skill associated with the club maker's art, it did herald the era of matching clubs, something that had been virtually impossible before.

It is interesting to see how the golf swing has been affected by the materials available for clubs and balls. Pictures of golfers up to the end of the last century show exactly what you would expect from a study of their equipment. A wooden club with a shaft length

J. H. Taylor advises aspiring golfers on the suitability of clubs in Harrods' sports department.

Laurie Auchterlonie, the famous St Andrews club maker, sits among exhibits in the museum that is attached to his shop.

The change of design to the bulger head also led to a different method of fixing the shaft. By drilling out the neck of the clubhead the shaft could safely be inserted and glued – a much simpler operation than the earlier scared joint and one which led directly to mass production.

At the same time iron clubs were gaining in popularity. Easier and cheaper to make than wooden heads, they could do little damage to the tougher gutta-percha ball, and they stood up much longer to hard usage.

of 45 in (1.14 m) and a 'very obtuse angle' between shaft and clubhead must produce a long, very flat swing. There was really no alternative in those days. Hazel shafts were just not strong enough to take heavy contact with the ground so our golfing ancestors adopted an open stance and swept the ball off the turf with long clubs and flat swings.

This type of swing, allied to golf balls which lacked the resilience of today's highly researched missiles, meant that the ball flew on a

much flatter trajectory. This put a premium on positional play to get near the pin on hard, dry greens – unlike today's game where the ball can be flown vast distances over any intervening hazards and stopped dead on heavily watered greens.

The advent of hickory shafts and the heavier gutta-percha ball brought about a shortening of club shafts, but swings were still relatively flat and divots were rarely taken, usually by accident. It was only with the advent of steel shafts in the 1920s that golf began to develop into the divot-digging, high-flying game it is today.

It is doubtful if golf would have survived at all and certain that it would not have become one of the world's most popular games if it had not been for three extraordinary advances in the design and manufacture of the humble golf ball.

There can have been very little pleasure in clouting a wooden golf ball with a crudely shaped piece of tree branch, so the golfers of the early 1600s must have been highly delighted when the 'featherie' ball first made its appearance. To them it must have seemed like a miracle of feel and control.

The featherie was notoriously difficult to make. Even a skilled ball maker like Allan Robertson, recognized as the first professional golfer, could not produce more than six in one full day's work, and often the total was only four. The ball was based, either consciously or unconsciously on that used by the Ancient Romans for their stick-and-ball game, known as *paganica* of which, unfortunately, no further details have survived.

The ball consisted of two or three shaped pieces of bull's hide which were soaked in alum water. They were stitched together, leaving a small gap for the essential filling to be applied and then turned inside out to give a smoother outer skin. Traditionally a top-hat full of goose feathers were boiled to reduce their bulk and were then stuffed into the hide cover. The ball maker would work first with hand implements, but as the ball neared completion he would have to resort to using a long iron brogue which was fitted with a cross-piece at the top so that extra pressure could be applied by putting it under the arm or against the chest.

As the wet leather dried out it shrank. Exactly the opposite was true of the feathers, which expanded rapidly as they dried. The resultant opposite pressures produced a ball which was remarkably hard and retained its shape reasonably well. Unfortunately it was very easily cut, was liable to split open at the seams when it got wet – and was extremely expensive.

With the next significant change, the development of the gutta-percha ball or 'guttie', in about 1848, came also the first practical lesson in aerodynamics. Because of the way they were made the featherie balls had slightly raised stitching and seams on their surface. But the new balls, made by heating a piece of gutta percha and clamping it in a mould, were much

A well-annotated page from the Illustrated Sporting and Dramatic News *of December 1908.*

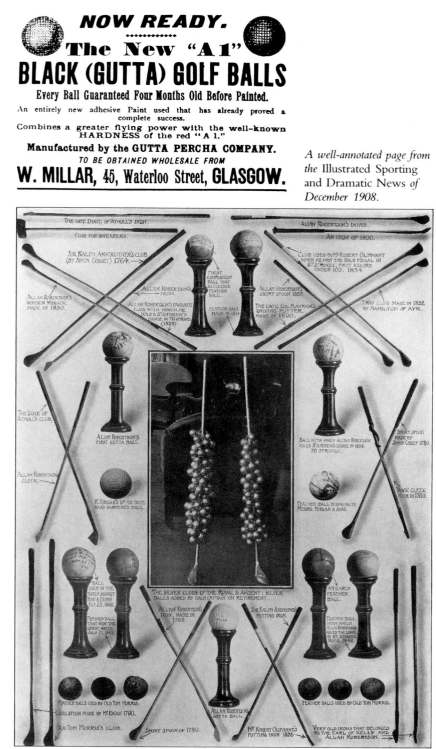

Allan Robertson (clubs under his arm) watches the captain of the R & A, Captain Frank Wemyss (c.1850). On the extreme left is Old Tom Morris and the boy is Jamie Anderson, later to win three successive Open Championships.

smoother – and in their perfect newly-made state they did not fly very well.

A new ball tended to dive very quickly into the ground, and only through trial and error was it noticed that a worn, scuffed ball flew further and straighter than a new one. This led the makers first to rough up the surface of the new ball and later to indent it with dimples. It is these small dimples which give a golf ball backspin and lift.

Allan Robertson was not at all amused by the arrival of the new ball. Claims that it flew further and lasted much longer filled him with despair for the future of his own featherie-making business. He actually paid local schoolboys to bring him any guttie balls they found so that he could burn them and, in some small way, halt their progress.

He would not allow any of his golf-ball makers to try the new ball, but the legendary Old Tom Morris, who had worked for him for many years, was caught in the embarrassing situation of losing all his featherie balls while playing the Old Course at St Andrews with a Mr Campbell. His partner gave him a guttie ball to try and Tom took to it at once. As they approached the final holes they passed Allan Robertson on the course and someone told him that Tom was playing a good game with one of the new balls.

In Tom's own words: 'I could see fine from the expression on his face that he did not like it at all, and, when we met afterwards in his shop, we had high words about the matter, and there and then we parted company, I leaving his employment.'

Robertson eventually gave in to progress and switched to making the gutta-percha ball, which was then selling at less than a

Sandy Herd, successful with the Haskell ball.

quarter the price of a featherie.

The exact date of the first gutta-percha ball is not known, but for many years it was believed to have been invented by a Rev Dr R. Paterson in St Andrews. He received a small Hindu statue from the Far East packed in chips and lumps of gutta-percha. The story goes that he made the packing material into a golf ball and first played with it alone one April morning in 1845. This version is now dismissed as fanciful nonsense, but it was certainly about this time that gutta-percha began to arrive in Britain – and the Hindu statue still exists in a Dundee museum, bequeathed to it by a Rev James Paterson.

The next tremendous stride in golf-ball manufacture, and the one which brings us right up to the present day, was the arrival of the Haskell wound ball from America at about the turn of the century. The ball consisted of a central core of pliable material wound round and round with hundreds of feet of stretched rubber thread and then covered with a skin of gutta-percha. The resilience and bounce of this new ball was far in excess of anything experienced before and not unnaturally players began hitting it much further. Initially it was not so easy to control on and around the greens as it had the unfortunate tendency to leap off the clubface.

But Sandy Herd won the Open Championship of 1902 with an imported Haskell ball, for which he paid about eight times the regular price because they were so scarce. He used the same ball for all four rounds and it was showing both signs of wear and part of its entrails by the time he won the title by one stroke from Harry Vardon and James Braid.

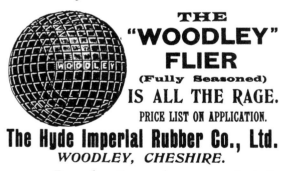

From that time on the new wonder ball was rapidly accepted by all levels of golfer, but ironically it had been invented in St Andrews by a retired Navy captain, Duncan Stewart, almost thirty years earlier. Constantly experimenting with golf balls, Stewart made and sold many gutta-percha balls to which he had added ground cork and iron filings. But the ball which he and a select band of his golfing companions liked best

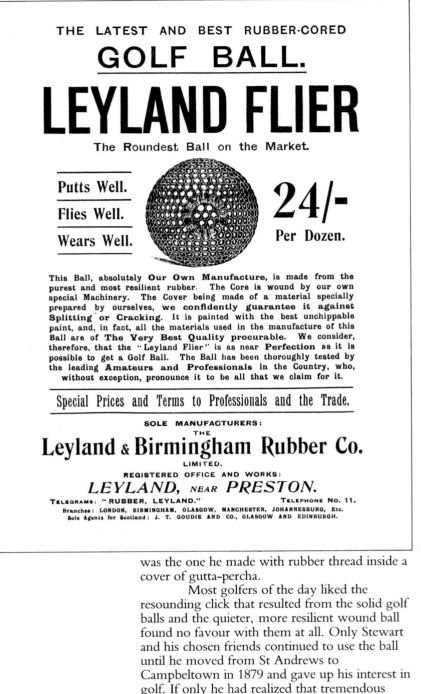
was the one he made with rubber thread inside a cover of gutta-percha.

Most golfers of the day liked the resounding click that resulted from the solid golf balls and the quieter, more resilient wound ball found no favour with them at all. Only Stewart and his chosen friends continued to use the ball until he moved from St Andrews to Campbeltown in 1879 and gave up his interest in golf. If only he had realized that tremendous commercial success and world-wide recognition were just around the corner. The ball which he invented in the 1870s in fact differs very little from the ball which is universally used today.

herever there was golf there was a tavern to which the wealthier golfers would retreat to settle wagers and arrange matches for the following week. Games would be played over common stretches of ground, often with an undignified scramble at the first tee and often interrupted by pedestrians, dogs and horses. In the earliest rules mention was made of balls being stopped by persons, horses and dogs – there was no relief, you merely played the ball from where it came to rest.

The tradition of 18 holes being a round of golf had not then been established and many of the early courses consisted of five, nine or 12 holes. Imagine the congestion on a five-hole course on a busy Saturday when three times over the same holes constituted a round.

It was on just such a course, the crowded Leith Links, that the Duke of York took part in a high-money challenge against two Englishmen. He chose as his partner an Edinburgh shoe-maker, John Pattersone, a renowned local golfer, who obviously carried his noble partner to a great victory. The exact amount of the wager was not recorded, but Pattersone was able to build a house in Edinburgh's Canongate with his share of the proceeds. He called his house Golfer's Land and the plaque which adorned the front wall and which bore the ultimate golfing legend, 'Far and

Sure', is still in place today.

As the game became more formalized, groups of golfers banded together to form their own societies or clubs. Initially these societies continued to use the local course and hostelry, but eventually they built their own clubhouses and finally moved away to private grounds with their own course.

One of the earliest landscape paintings featuring golf is a marvellous watercolour by Paul Sandby in 1746 showing the Bruntsfield Links, situated on high ground on the southern edge of Edinburgh with views of the dominating castle. This is where members of the Royal Burgess Society played their golf and part of that original course is still preserved as a par-three course in the heart of the city today. So, too, is the Golf Tavern, built in 1456.

At the time that Sandby completed his painting a club servant spent the first part of each Saturday morning calling at the houses of all members to inquire if they wished to dine in their private room at the Tavern that evening. Members would either walk or take their horse-drawn carriages or traps to the links. Dress for the game itself was an obligatory red jacket and fines were readily imposed on members failing to observe this ritual.

Golf was almost always played in the form of singles or foursomes matches. Each golfer would have a caddy, who would carry the clubs, not in a bag, but as a loose bundle under

Inside the clubhouse at Lytham & St Annes in 1893.

his arm. He would also have at least half a dozen featherie golf balls about his person, maybe many more, depending upon the ability of his master, for they were very easily split and just as easily lost. Wagers most often took the form of whisky or wine – another reason why the post-match dinners were so convivial and popular.

Captaincy of the club was decided by winning the annual championship, and the captain presided at every dinner. Those gathered around him would now be wearing the more traditional evening jackets of blue or grey and would soon need to loosen the gilt buttons as they demolished vast quantities of venison, beef, mutton and pigeon pie – not selecting one item from the menu as today's polite society demands, but following one with another and washing it all down with copious draughts of wine. Tobias Smollett recorded that club golfers rarely retired to bed with less than a gallon of claret in their bellies.

But that was by no means the end of the entertainment. During the course of the meal the club's recorder would bring out the book in which he had faithfully taken note of the previous Saturday evening's barely comprehensible challenges and ever bolder wagers. Once those had been settled by the handing over of the odd gallon of liquid assets, the whole process would start over again. The winners would undoubtedly break open their spoils and it was a wonder that anyone was ready for golf again seven days later.

The poor lad who had woken the members that morning and taken orders for dinner had also acted as a caddie in the afternoon and helped to serve the meal at night. In the mid-18th century the faithful servant who carried out these duties for the Burgess Society in Edinburgh was paid six shillings a quarter and given a suit of clothes 'to be worn only on Saturday and Sunday'. Ten years later he was also voted a pair of shoes at the society's expense 'on account of the large increase of members which occasioned a great deal of additional walking'.

As with the beginnings of the game itself it is extremely difficult to pinpoint exact dates when societies of this kind first came into being, but certainly after the gentlemen golfers of Leith made their request to Edinburgh City Council for a silver club in 1744 a great many clubs and societies started to keep detailed records of their affairs. There seems no doubt, however, that the golfers of Leith and Bruntsfield were the first to form themselves into recognized societies; certainly they were well in advance of any such movement in St Andrews which now enjoys the world-wide reputation of being the 'Home of Golf'.

How good were those early golfers? Despite their rather crude clubs and featherie balls they played a more powerful and sophisticated game than most people imagine. The famous links at Leith consisted of five holes which measured 414, 461, 426, 495 and 435 yards. Good players could hit the ball 200 yards, so each hole, in effect, was a good-sized par five. Three times round was a normal game and the average score worked out at about six and a half strokes per hole.

Any takers for next Saturday? A gallon of claret to the winners!

Douglas Robertson, five times winner of the Gold Medal of the Royal and Ancient Golf Club and on three occasions winner of the Gold Medal of the Honourable Company of Edinburgh Golfers in the 1860s and 1870s.

Facing page
John Taylor, captain of the Edinburgh Golfers for eight years between 1807 and 1825.

RULES AND REGULATIONS

OF

THE HONOURABLE COMPANY OF EDINBURGH GOLFERS

I. That the Name of the Club shall be "THE HONOURABLE COMPANY OF EDINBURGH GOLFERS."

II. The Club shall consist of not more than Five Hundred Members, exclusive of Life Members and those on the Supernumerary List. The number of Members may be from time to time altered, under such conditions as the Club shall in General Meeting prescribe.

Number of Members.

III. Every Candidate for admission shall be proposed by one Member and seconded by another. His name and address must be sent, with the names of his proposer and seconder, to the Secretary, by filling up the official Form, at least three weeks previous to the ballot. No Candidate shall be proposed for admission until he shall have attained the age of fifteen, and no Candidate shall be eligible for election until he shall have attained the age of nineteen. Vacancies shall be filled by ballot at a General Meeting to be held on the Second Thursday in February and/or such other dates as the Committee may fix. Ballots shall be held under the following Regulations :

Admission.

1st. A List of the names and designations of the several Candidates, with the names of their respective proposers and seconders, shall be placed on the notice board in the Club-

---

18

BEDROOM REGULATIONS.

I. A Bedroom may be reserved by a Member for any specific date named by him, preference being given according to priority of application.

II. A Member shall be entitled to occupy a Bedroom for seven consecutive nights unless it has been reserved by a previous application. Members who have occupied Rooms for such term shall be liable to be dispossessed should an application for a Bedroom be received before *One p.m. on the following day.* The occupant of the oldest date shall be the first to be dispossessed.

III. The Club Steward shall keep a book, subject to the inspection of Members, wherein he shall enter all applications for Bedrooms, together with the day and hour in which each was received. The preference shall be always due to the priority of such date ; but in case of more than one application being received at the same time for the same night, the preference shall be given to the Member who has been the longest period without occupying a Bedroom ; and where no such distinction exists, then to the senior Member of the Club.

IV. A Member for whom a Bedroom has been reserved shall pay for it whether he occupies it or not, unless he has given notice to the Club Steward before *Twelve o'clock noon on the day prior to that for which the Bedroom was reserved.*

V. In every case a Member shall intimate to the Club Steward his intention of giving up his Room *before One o'clock on the day of his departure* (at which hour his luggage may be removed if necessary), or he shall pay for the Room for that night.

Charge per night, 5s.
Charge for Fire in Bedroom if lighted at 5 P.M., 1s. ; if lighted in the morning, 1s. extra.
Charge for a Bath after 10 A.M., 1s.

Reprinted *April 1928.*

John Reid, the founding father of US golf.

Top *Harvard & Yale play host to a team from Oxford & Cambridge at the Myopia Hunt Club in 1903.*
Centre *The elegant Myopia clubhouse.*
Bottom *Golf at the Meadowbrook Golf Club at Hempstead on Long Island in 1899.*

t has long been accepted that a Scot, John Reid, was the man who started golf in America when he invited neighbours at Yonkers-on-the-Hudson, New York, to sample his native game on a stretch of meadowland opposite his home. This game took place on 22 February 1888, and was timed to celebrate George Washington's birthday.

Reid had lived in America since he was a youngster, but in late 1887 he asked a friend, Bob Lockhart, who was making a trip to Scotland, to bring back a few golf clubs. Washington's birthday the following year was their first public outing and he gave an exhibition over three improvised holes with John Upham.

Four neighbours showed an immediate interest and by November of that year Reid called his friends together at a dinner party and the St Andrews Golf Club was formally brought into being. In the present clubhouse of the St Andrews Golf Club – now at Hastings-on-Hudson – a bronze plaque reads:

John Reid
Scotsman – American
The Founder of St Andrews Golf Club and its
first President
Born in 1840 at Dunfermline, Scotland. Died in
1916 at Yonkers–on–Hudson,
New York.
A lover of men, of books, of sports; a loyal
friend, a rare interpreter
of the songs of his native land.

John Reid's portrait hangs in the headquarters of the United States Golf Association in Far Hills, New Jersey. Reid has come to be regarded as the father of American golf, and in many respects he was just that. No other club has records going back as far, and no other club has remained in existence longer.

However, golf was played in America at least a hundred years earlier. There is a reference to the formation of a golf club at Charleston in a 1786 edition of the *South Carolina and Georgia Almanac*. There are further mentions in newspaper reports in 1788, and biographical records of local people mention the playing of golf at Harleston Green, Charleston in 1791.

Just across the state line at Savannah, Georgia, there are references to a golf club being brought into being before 1800 and continuing

Facing page *Charles Blair Macdonald, the first 'official' US Amateur champion.*

until the start of the War of 1812. It was at this same time that all references to golf in Charleston disappeared from the records. It was to be many years before golf was again played in America. When it did re-appear – and there are counter-claims for the title of earliest golf club from Dorset Fields in Vermont (1886) and Foxburg Country Club, Pennsylvania (1887) which rival the St Andrews Club (1888) – it spread at an incredible rate with more than one thousand courses being brought into existence by the turn of the century.

Unfortunately over six hundred of the early courses built in America were the work of the first recorded confidence trickster in the game. This vast disservice was done to American golf by Tom Bendelow, and was unravelled by golf writer Charles Price.

Bendelow worked as a compositor on a New York newspaper. His broad Scottish accent convinced many unsuspecting Americans that he had a vast knowledge of the ancient game. In fact he knew very little about golf, but a lot about getting a stranglehold on a growing market. He became a golf-course architect and his ability to design new courses at the breathtaking pace of one a day is not as impressive as it sounds. They were all identical!

He would drive a stake into the ground to locate the first tee, pace out a hundred yards and mark out that spot as a cross bunker, another hundred yards and he would stake out a mound the shape of a chocolate drop, and a further hundred yards gave him the location of the green. Here he did allow himself a little variety – his greens were either completely circular or square. There were no features or hazards. At $25 for each course he made a small fortune, and created a great deal of work for local farmers who were soon called in to plough up his efforts.

Despite the fact that a Scot tried his hardest to ruin the spread of his national game in America, golf survived the Bendelow treatment and rapidly flourished. Even so, early attempts to organize an amateur championship were marked by disputes, many of which involved Charles Blair Macdonald, an American who had studied at St Andrews University. He found fault with every event he did not win. When he was beaten into second place in the first attempt at a championship, organized in 1893 by Newport Golf Club over 36 holes of stroke-play, he insisted that only match-play was a

proper way to decide such an important event. But when St Andrews staged such a match-play championship in 1894, he again finished second saying that it was not a properly run championship, and it was largely due to his vociferous outpourings that five of the oldest established clubs got together to form the Amateur Golf Association of the United States, later to become the United States Golf Association.

The five clubs were St Andrews, Newport, Shinnecock Hills, The Country Club at Brookline, Massachusetts, and the Chicago Golf Club. Through an oversight the Tuxedo Club of New York was left out of the original line-up, and this caused a certain amount of friction since the Tuxedo Club had as much claim to be a founder member as the others.

From 1895 the American Amateur and Open Championships have been staged under the auspices of the USGA and, yes, Macdonald finally did win the American Amateur Championship in that very year. It was, perhaps, a small price to pay for his silence.

The Open Championship is a mammoth production costing £1.5 million, attracting a massive entry of the world's greatest players, taking months to set up and offering prize-money currently totalling £650,000.

It all began much more modestly. The first Championship, organized in 1860 by the Prestwick Golf Club on the Ayrshire coast of Scotland, was contested by only eight players over three rounds of the 12-hole course. Willie Park of Musselburgh won the handsome belt of red Moroccan leather with its large silver buckle. His score was 174, two shots better than Old Tom Morris, the renowned St Andrews professional who had moved to Prestwick nine years previously. Park's score represents two rounds of 87, not too disastrous with the equipment of the day and in the bad weather that marred the event.

Old Tom got his revenge the following year with a score of 163 and was to win the Championship four times before his son, Tom

The plaque at Prestwick which commemorates the first Open Championship. Below Willie Park, Junior (centre) who followed his father's footsteps and became Open Champion in 1887 and 1889.

Morris Junior, swept everyone aside in 1868, the first of his four consecutive victories before he died tragically young. With a remarkable score of 149 in 1870 he secured the Championship belt as his own property and successfully retained his title when the Championship resumed after a year's absence in 1872, this time for the familiar silver claret jug which is still presented annually to the winner.

The number of contestants during the first 12 years of the Open, when it was held permanently at Prestwick, never reached more than 17. Once, in 1864, it fell as low as six. In that respect it was not truly representative, although enough of the very best players always

Left Old Tom Morris (left) and his son who dominated the early years of the Open. Facing page Left Walter J. Travis, the first American to win the Amateur Championship in 1904. Right British Ladies' Champion Mrs Dorothy Campbell takes a drop at the US Ladies' Championship during her visit to the United States in 1909.

The climax of the 1895 Open.
Top *Andrew Kirkaldy who took third place.*
Centre *Alexander Herd, the runner-up.*
Bottom *J.H. Taylor playing the winning stroke on the final green.*

Facing page
Mr Balfour drives in as captain of the R & A in 1894.

managed to compete for the credibility of the Open to survive.

The reason for these small entries was simply Prestwick's location. Virtually all the other leading clubs and courses were on Scotland's east coast between Aberdeen and Edinburgh, and the journey through to the west was long and expensive. From 1873 three clubs took it in turn to host the Championship – Prestwick, Musselburgh and St Andrews – where the entry was always significantly higher, 82 players taking part there in 1891 compared with only 40 at Prestwick the previous year. Eventually a consortium of some 26 clubs ran the Championship but then in 1919 they voted unanimously to hand over the management of the Amateur and Open Championships to the sole care of the Royal and Ancient Golf Club of St Andrews.

In some ways that decision at the end of the First World War went a long way to setting the record straight, for St Andrews had organized three Grand National Tournaments, open to all gentlemen players, in the three years preceding the first Open at Prestwick. These Grand Tournaments were clear forerunners of the Amateur Championship which did not become established until 1885. But, to be fair, even this idea had been put forward by Prestwick.

It was not just the superior location which clinched the decision to hold the Grand Tournaments in St Andrews in the years 1857 – 59. Almost a hundred years earlier the 22-hole course had been adjusted to 18 holes. In the 1850s Prestwick had 12 holes, Musselburgh nine and North Berwick only seven. In addition, the St Andrews course had been in play for hundreds of years while other courses were relatively new or had been established for some time but had moved to new golfing grounds. It was, in fact, in 1858 that the following entry was written into the rules of the R & A: 'One round of the links, or eighteen holes, is reckoned a match.'

In exercising control of the world's oldest championship and in having custodianship of the game's laws the Royal and Ancient Golf Club has a position unequalled in golf. Its beginnings were much more humble and its rise to a position of eminence quite remarkable.

It all started in 1754 when, following the example of the Gentlemen Golfers at Leith, who formed themselves into an official society

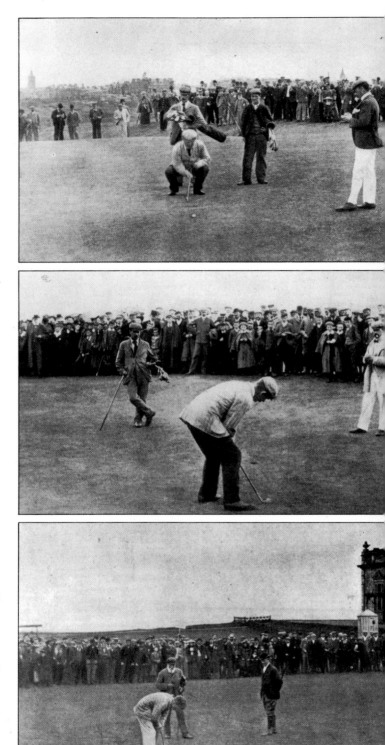

and were responsible for the first written rules of the game 10 years earlier, a total of 22 noblemen and gentlemen of the Kingdom of Fife banded together to create the Society of St Andrews Golfers. At that time it was just another private golf club, concerned solely with its own members and competitions. There was no clubhouse, dinners and meetings being held either at the Black Bull Tavern or at Baillie Glass's establishment. Golf was played, in common with other local golfers, over the links of St Andrews.

In 1834 King William IV became the club's patron and bestowed the rather more grand title Royal and Ancient Golf Club of St Andrews. The following year the club agreed to share the premises of the Union Club overlooking the 18th green and jointly raised £800 for the building of the present clubhouse in 1854. The two clubs officially amalgamated in 1877 and silver bearing the Union Club name is still in daily use in the R & A dining room.

As the golfers of St Andrews were enjoying their improving status, their more senior counterparts at Leith were experiencing difficult times. As the compilers of the first rules of golf and the most senior club their advice on golfing tradition and law was constantly in demand. In time the five-hole course at Leith became impossibly crowded and the Gentlemen Golfers of Leith – now under the new title of the Honorable Company of Edinburgh Golfers – moved to the nine-hole course at nearby Musselburgh. But again a move was forced on them, this time much farther east to their present course at Muirfield.

A certain loss of identity and direction was inevitable during this period, while at the same time the St Andrews golfers were firmly established and had acquired the further distinction of royal approval. Subtly but inexorably the balance of power began to shift from Edinburgh to St Andrews. It was not a transfer of authority that was either planned or sought-after, merely a change in emphasis brought about over a lengthy period.

Thus, by the time the leading clubs were seeking a uniform code of rules towards the end of the century the R & A had become the natural choice to undertake such a task. In 1897 they appointed the first Rules of Golf Committee and to this day are responsible for the administration of rules throughout the world, with the exception of the United States

(6)

5. PENALTIES. — Any person who shall contravene any of the foregoing bye-laws shall be liable, on conviction, in a penalty not exceeding one pound for each offence, and, failing payment, to imprisonment for any period not exceeding fourteen days.

St Andrews, 20th March 1897.—Allowed and confirmed, as altered and initialled.

(Signed) Æ. J. G. MACKAY,
Sheriff of Fife.

I hereby approve the foregoing Bye-Laws.

(Signed) BALFOUR OF BURLEIGH,
Secretary for Scotland.

SCOTTISH OFFICE,
WHITEHALL, *10th April 1897.*

(7)

REGULATIONS FOR STARTING

MADE BY

THE GREEN COMMITTEE OF ST ANDREWS LINKS, UNDER THE POWERS CONFERRED ON THEM BY THE ST ANDREWS LINKS ACT, 1894, AND APPROVED OF BY THE BURGH COMMISSIONERS OF ST ANDREWS ON 23RD FEBRUARY 1898.

1. When a Starter is employed, he will be present from 9 a.m. till 5 p.m., and shall start the players in accordance with the times in the Time Table, and with Rules Nos. 6 and 7.

2. On these occasions applications for starting must be made by card, which must be placed in the Starter's box, or in a box at the Post Office, not later than 5 p.m. the previous day, and for a Monday, not later than 5 p.m. on the previous Saturday. Application may also be made by post cards or telegrams (addressed to " Starter, St Andrews ") which will be treated in the same way as the cards. The cards, post cards, and telegrams shall each afternoon be mixed and ballotted, and effect given to the hour applied for in the order in which they come out at the ballot. Should the hour named be already

ROYAL & ANCIENT GOLF CLUB HOUSE . ST ANDREWS

WATCHING THE PLAYERS

OLD TOM MORRIS

Golf at St Andrews as seen by the Illustrated Sporting and Dramatic News *in 1889.*

and Mexico who are governed by the United States Golf Association. However, regular meetings are held between the two bodies and a uniform set of world-wide rules exists as a consequence.

What those original 22 noblemen and Gentlemen of Fife would have thought of the R & A's unique position in world golf today is impossible to imagine, but the old club has certainly come a long way since its first meetings in the back room of the Black Bull Tavern.

30

ispute over prize-money, or rather the lack of it, at Open Championships in the closing years of the 19th century was one of the key factors which led to the formation of the Professional Golfers' Association. Yet by the time the pros had banded themselves together as an official body in 1901, their aims and intentions were far wider-ranging.

The Honorable Company of Edinburgh Golfers had recently moved to their present

their clubs. Many worked for small, poor clubs which could not afford to pay even a reasonable retaining fee and others were attached to the powerful clubs which could demand almost impossible hours and conditions of work. Worst of all, many clubs were investigating the possibility of selling clubs and balls directly to their members without involving the professional.

This had become a possibility in recent years since the beginnings of mass production. Before that most golf equipment was made by

The early professionals – some great names of their day. Left to right: J.H. Taylor, H. Vardon, W. Auchterlonie, A. Kirkaldy, W. Fernie, J. Braid, G. Causey, B. Sayers.

course at Muirfield before the Open of 1892, and they announced their intention of staging that year's Championship on the new course for the standard prize fund of £30. The residents and golfers of Musselburgh, where six previous Opens had been held when it was the home of the Honorable Company, were horrified by this paltry sum. Led by local hero Willie Park, the local business people put up £100 for a rival event to be held on the same date. The Honorable Company bowed to this pressure and suddenly produced £110 in prize-money, and the Musselburgh event was played the day after the Open.

Seven years later, on the eve of the Open at Sandwich in Kent, a large group of professionals threatened strike action if there was not a substantial increase in the purse they were to play for, which had stayed at around the £100 mark. Thankfully the wise counsel of Taylor, Vardon, Braid and Park intervened and they negotiated a £30 increase.

Of equal importance to the pros at this time was the way they were being treated by

J.H. Taylor on the tee.

the professionals themselves in their own workshops. If clubs had persisted with their idea it would have made it impossible for the pros to making even a poor living at the game. In J.H. Taylor the professionals had the perfect man to fight for their rights. He had won the first of his

five Open titles in 1894 and through sheer
determination had become an accomplished
writer and public speaker after the poorest of
starts, leaving school at the age of eleven to help
support his widowed mother. He was a man of
enormous integrity who was respected not only
by his fellow professionals but by everyone
connected with the game of golf.

He discussed the problems at length
with Harold Hilton, a distinguished amateur
who had become editor of *Golf Illustrated*, and he
published a leading article on the subject in
March 1901. There followed a spate of
correspondence and, at a meeting held in
Paternoster lane behind St Paul's Cathedral at the
beginning of September, the London and
Counties Professional Golfers' Association came
into being with fifty immediate members.

Their constitution was simply stated:
'The object of the Association shall be to
promote interest in the game of golf; to protect
and advance the mutual and trade interests of all
members; to hold meetings and tournaments
periodically for the encouragement of the
younger members; to act as an agency for
assisting any professional or club maker to
obtain employment; and to effect any other
objects of a like nature as may be determined
from time to time by the Association.'

Their first event was played for a mere
£15 worth of prizes in October that same year at
Tooting Bec Golf Club. Taylor himself won the
first prize of £5 and the cup which was presented
by the club. This trophy is now awarded anually
to the PGA member with the lowest single-
round score in the Open Championship.

From those small beginnings the
Association has grown to a strength of more
than 3,500 members with a national
headquarters, six regional offices and the PGA
European Tour for tournament players. Yet,
despite the tremendous strides that have been
made over the past nine decades, attitudes from a
century and a half ago still linger.

The first professionals were often
uneducated men who shirked responsibility but
had some prowess at the game of golf. Their
living was precarious: they earned a few shillings
from playing with amateurs and trying to teach
them the rudiments of the game, and they often
acted as caddies when there was no better money
to be earned. Some were club and ball makers,
and a rare few were intelligent enough and held
in high-enough esteem to be made Keepers of
the Green. These men were paid a salary by the
club, were responsible for the condition of the
course and for controlling the caddies and
professionals. They were usually provided with
a workshop where they would employ club and
ball makers.

However, the vast majority of
professionals were rough-and-ready men, little
better than caddies, and very much servants of
the wealthy amateur players. As late as the 1940s
many club professionals – by now highly
respectable citizens in every way – were still not
allowed inside the clubhouse of even their home
club, and had to collect their lunch from the
kitchen door.

By contrast, those good players who
went off in their hundreds to America were
treated like gods. The ability to play the game

A golfing weekend for Mr A.W. Gamage (standing, left) and his guest Colonel Western (standing, right) who had retained the services of two leading professionals, Harry Vardon (seated, left) and J.H. Taylor (seated, right).

and a general knowledge of the layout and upkeep of courses made them invaluable. They were usually sponsored by one of the wealthiest members of the clubs which employed them and they swiftly moved into the upper social circles.

While the British golf professional is largely well respected today he is still regarded as something of a club servant. His counterpart in America is accorded much greater credibility and is expected to help shape club policy and to take a major part in the overall control of his club. Historic roots are hard to shake off.

Changing social attitudes have passed across the history of golf as cloud shadows flit over a sunlit course. They may have made a temporary impression but they have left the game remarkably untouched and true to its original concept. Despite these ever-shifting attitudes and regular changes in equipment and courses, the basic rules and the way in which golf is played are very close today to the game that was played in the 1440s.

In those far-off days it was undoubtedly the fisherman and the artisan who first took to the game, fashioning their own clubs and balls from wood. But it was not long before the wealthy merchants and noblemen began to take a keen interest in the new sport. Their money enabled them to buy clubs fashioned lovingly by craftsmen who more normally were producing bows and arrows.

It was the ability of these new converts to the game to pay for better equipment that led to the development of the featherie ball and the advances in club design. The fisherfolk and the blacksmith still continued to play the game over the same stretches of golfing country as their more wealthy counterparts and they eventually began to benefit from the improved equipment as they acquired the odd discarded club and picked up the featherie balls which were lost in their hundreds in the gorse and heather which encroached closely on the fairways.

Inevitably the wealthier patrons of the game, now heavily sprinkled with royalty, developed the desire to create their own clubs and ultimately their own courses. Yet in most of the areas of east Scotland where the game began, noble members of those early clubs continued to play over the same links as the rest of the population even after they had built their own clubhouses.

Golf first spread out of Scotland with James VI when he also assumed control of the fractious hordes on the other side of Hadrian's Wall as James I of England. Away from its native links the game slowly began to assume a different and more élitist character. By Victorian times the rapid expansion of golf was almost entirely through private clubs and courses to which the local artisans had no access. Unfortunately it was this socially limited form of the game that the Victorian empire-builders exported and imposed on countries such as India and parts of Africa, along with many other unsavoury aspects of their blinkered lifestyle.

Only in Scotland did the game remain true to its origins throughout this period. Certainly, wealthy élitist clubs were formed even here, but they were matched by an equal number of clubs which catered, if in more modest fashion, for the golfing and social needs of the working man. Also in Scotland there was still contact and golfing rivalry between members of the grandest and most humble clubs – many of whom continued to share the same public courses.

Victorian snobbishness did golf two great disservices: first by keeping the game away from the great mass of the population and secondly, in later years, by discriminating against golfers from working-class backgrounds who, however excellent as players, were by-passed for national team selection on social rather than golfing considerations.

There have always been, however, men who were able to span any divides that appeared in the game – men of dignity, ability and vision. Perhaps the first and most notable was Old Tom Morris. Born in St Andrews in 1821 he became a ball maker with Allan Robertson, universally recognized as the first professional. Tom's skill as a golfer matched and probably surpassed that of his employer for Robertson protected his

Harry Vardon drives off the 1st tee during the 1900 Open at St Andrews under the watchful eye of Old Tom Morris.

reputation as a player by judiciously avoiding encounters which he might lose. Old Tom added a bushy beard to his already large frame and was an imposing figure throughout his life. After a spell at Prestwick as Keeper of the Green he returned to St Andrews to become

Former champions Harry Vardon (putting) and J.H. Taylor contest the minor places in the 1901 Open while (below) James Braid sinks the putt which gave the Championship back to Scotland for the first time since 1893.

professional and to have full charge of the links for an annual salary of £50. His gifted son, Tom Morris Junior, won the first of his four Opens at the age of 18, having first played in the Championship four years earlier.

In 1875 father and son were taking part in a challenge match at North Berwick when a telegram was handed to Old Tom saying that his son's wife had died in childbirth. A private yacht was put at their disposal to carry them across the entrance to the Firth of Forth and save them the longer journey by rail through Edinburgh. It was only as they entered St Andrews harbour that Old Tom broke the full tragedy of the news to his son. In just over three months, on Christmas morning, Young Tom was found dead at his home at the age of 24.

Old Tom was destined to outlive his two sons and his daughter. He died in 1908 after falling down a flight of steps at the New Club in St Andrews just a month short of his 87th birthday. On the day of his funeral no golf was played in St Andrews.

On New Year's Day, 1886 Tom Morris was in philosophical mood as he confided to a fellow golfer: 'Had it not been for golf I'm not sure that at this day I would have been still a living man. I've had my troubles like the rest, and my sorrows, so that at times to lie down and die looked all that was left for me. But with the help of God and of golf, I have managed to survive.' That fellow golfer was A.J. Balfour and it was a measure of Old Tom's character that the local man from humble beginnings could converse so easily and openly with the man who was soon to become Prime Minister. It speaks volumes for Tom Morris and for the game of golf.

Another in the same mould who followed him successfully through the turn of the century and into the ever-expanding years beyond was J.H. Taylor, five times Open Champion, self-taught writer and orator and founding father of the Professional Golfers' Association. The same era threw up Harry Vardon, the phlegmatic Channel Islander who first brought the overlapping grip to the attention of the world, and who was a six-time winner of the Open Championship. Probably closest to the character of Old Tom Morris was fellow Fifer James Braid, a man of quiet presence and dignity who was also five times an Open winner.

Together Vardon, Braid and Taylor

took 16 Open titles over a 20-year span. Where Arnold Palmer, Jack Nicklaus and Gary Player became known as the Big Three in the 1960s, the more flowery language of the earlier age christened Vardon, Braid and Taylor the Great Triumvirate. In many ways this was an injustice to another St Andrean, Sandy Herd, who won the Championship only once but finished second no less than four times, the last time when he was well into his fifties.

Women have flitted in and out of the history of the game since its beginnings. Mary Queen of Scots was perhaps the first, being publicly criticized for playing golf the day after the death of her second husband, her young cousin Lord Darnley. It was even suggested that her callous behaviour indicated complicity in his murder – and most probably it did.

Although there are occasional references to competitions played among the women fishing folk at Musselburgh in about 1810, there appears to have been little interest in golf at this social level and certainly by the time ladies' clubs began to appear in the second half of the 19th century it was very much a genteel game played over very short courses in a garden-party atmosphere. How could it be much else in an

A tribute to The Great Triumvirate together with Sandy (or Alec) Herd, so often added to their number by writers of the day.

Arnaud Massy, the first competitor from across the Channel to win the Open Championship in 1907. Far left Mary Queen of Scots on the links at St Andrews in 1563.

age when voluminous dresses swept the ground. Before any full shot every lady had to capture her skirts in an elastic belt.

Lord Wellwood, an avid golfer and historian of the 1880s and 1890s, dismissed ladies' golf with a few patronizing words: 'We venture to suggest seventy or eighty yards as the average limit of a drive advisedly; not because we doubt a lady's power to make a longer drive, but because that cannot well be done without raising the club above the shoulder. Now, we do not presume to dictate, but we must observe that the posture and gestures requisite for a full swing are not particularly graceful when the player is clad in female dress.'

It was not long, however, before ladies began to raise their clubs well above shoulder height. After the formation of the Ladies' Golf Union in 1893 Lady Margaret Scott, daughter of the Earl of Eldon, won the first three British Ladies' Championships, but the most celebrated female golfer in the early days of the 20th century was undoubtedly Cecil Leitch, who reached the semi-finals of the Ladies' Open in 1908 at the tender age of 17, represented England for almost twenty years from 1910 and won the first of her four Championships in 1914.

Competitors in the first Ladies' Championship at St Annes in 1893.

Contestants on the green during the Ladies' Championship at Portrush in 1903.

One of the early visitors from the United States: Miss Higgins powers her way out of the rough during the Ladies' Championship at Troon in 1904.

Cecil Leitch and Harold Hilton during the first half of their challenge match. Right Lady golfers of the day would not have been too sympathetic to the activities of the Suffragette Movement in 1913.

At the age of 19 she accepted a challenge from Harold Hilton, four times Amateur Champion and twice winner of the Open, in the sort of match which attracted great attention and public debate. Played in 1910 over 72 holes at Walton Heath and Sunningdale, it was a struggle watched by more than four thousand people as Miss Leitch came from five down in the final round to win by 2 and 1. By way of handicap she was given the half, but over the final 17 holes of play she scored 77 to Hilton's 75. The age of women's golf had arrived.

After five hundred years of continuous play in its native east of Scotland, golf had spread by the early years of the 20th century to many countries of the world, to North America, through Britain and Europe and many parts of the Far East. It was flourishing at amateur and professional levels and yet the inherent qualities and attractions of the game had survived intact.

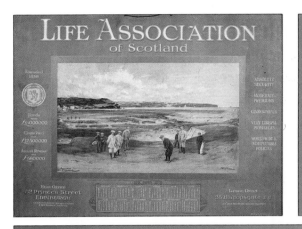

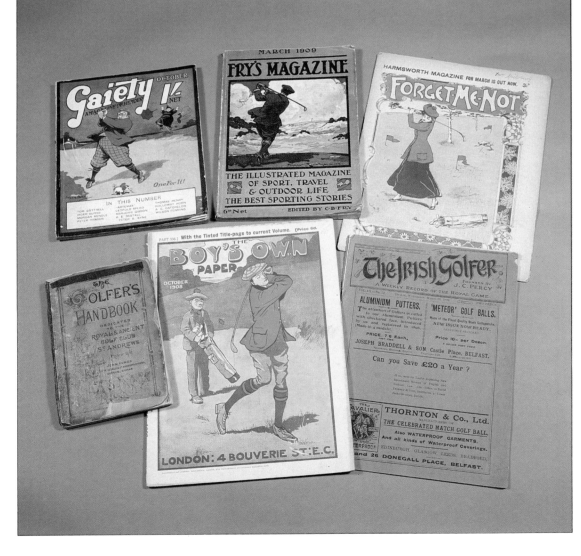

Golf featured prominently in all aspects of life at the turn of the century.
Left Comics, magazines and an early Golfer's Handbook.
Above Golfing labels for games, cigarettes and meat extract.
Above left A calendar for 1913 issued by the Life Association.

*Inside the home of golf —
the clubhouse of the Royal
and Ancient Golf Club of
St Andrews.*
Right *Crested notepaper
available to members in the
library.*
Far right *The trophy safe.*

*A showcase in the R & A
museum.*

The first winner's medal, presented to Young Tom Morris after the 1872 Open Championship.

Above left *Scales for weighing letters and (left) scales for weighing members in the gentlemen's lavatory.*

Popular golfing games for all the family.

PART TWO

GOLF BETWEEN TWO WARS,
1919–1939

Abe Mitchell (left) with Samuel Ryder, founder of the Ryder Cup. Far right George Duncan.

et us look first at the outward and visible changes in the appearance of the men who played the game. Always, before the First World War, photographs show the top golfers, amateur and professional, wearing jackets, and frequently plus-fours, and this stringency still persisted for a good few years afterwards. Clothes were rather drab until Walter Hagen was among the first to appear in bright colours in the 1920s, and was shortly copied by others. By the 1930s the professionals were playing in pullovers – Henry Cotton, for example, never played in a jacket.

At club level, golfers played in their oldest clothes, which they bundled into their lockers at the end of the round, with never a thought to preserving a crease in their trousers. Footwear was stout walking shoes with tackets, generally in threes, knocked into them. Hagen, again, was one of the first to wear black and white or brown and white shoes.

Hagen, who made fortunes, and spent them just about as rapidly, said of himself: 'I don't want to be a millionaire, I just want to live like one.' His influence on the game was a great

Henry Cotton (driving) and Walter Hagen at Muirfield in 1929. The jackets have gone but the ties remain.

deal more than cosmetic, since he did more than any man to raise the standing of the professional golfer. As one of his great rivals, Gene Sarazen, said of him: 'All the professionals who have a chance to go after the big money today should say a silent thanks to Walter each time they stretch a cheque between their fingers.'

When he first came to Britain, it was not customary for the professionals to lunch in the clubhouse. This made no sense to Hagen who drove in the thin edge of the wedge by arriving at the course in a hired Rolls-Royce and having a man-servant dispense a champagne lunch in front of the clubhouse windows.

The Twenties and Thirties were a breezy and, literally, fast-moving period in the history of golf. One of the greatest, and least welcome, changes between pre-1939 golf and its lame-duck form after 1945 is the time taken to play even a friendly round. In the old days it took about two and a half hours, nowadays it is nearer four. 'Shoot or drop the gun,' young players were told, and they also learned to be thinking of their next shot while the other fellow was playing his. In those days, too, handling the ball was kept to a minimum. Play the ball as it lies, that was the way. One of the greatest time-wasters of modern golf is the rule that allows the ball to be marked, lifted and cleaned before every putt. Players do it now even with a six-inch putt! Such dreariness would not have been tolerated in the age of Hagen and Cotton.

Immediately after the First World War the top professionals in Britain were George Duncan and Abe Mitchell. Duncan, born in Methlick, Aberdeenshire, in 1883 was 36 when golf resumed and Mitchell, born at East Grinstead in 1887, was 32. Duncan and Mitchell, Mitchell and Duncan, became to Britain as a pair what the Great Triumvirate of Vardon, Braid and Taylor had been as a trio.

They travelled extensively, played countless exhibition matches and contested together. As golfers they were poles apart. Duncan's book, *Golf at the Gallop,* had an apt title for a mercurial, temperamental genius who played so quickly that the stroke was frequently over before the crowds had time to settle. Mitchell was stolid and reserved, but grasping the club in a pair of massive hands, and with little apparent effort, he gave the ball a tremendous clout with arms, hands and wrists.

In 1920, in the first serious tournament after the war, over the famous Old Course at St

Andrews, Mitchell and Duncan tied and the golfing world agreed that there could have been no more fitting result. After this warm-up they went to Deal for the first post-war Open and Mitchell's opening 74 and 73 saw him six strokes ahead of the field and 13 in front of Duncan's two rounds of 80.

In those days, the Championship was completed in three days, having been increased from two days in 1904. A proper draw was made and the leaders did not automatically go out last. That arrangement was not introduced until 1957. Duncan, an early starter, finished his third round in 71, minutes before Mitchell set off.

Mitchell opened with three putts. More strokes slipped away and he had a seven at the 5th. He then had to endure a long delay while players piled up at the 6th. Eventually he finished in 84 and every stroke of his huge lead over Duncan had gone. Duncan completed his

final round in 72, a great day's golf in those times, and emerged as the winner with a total of 303. Mitchell with a final round of 76 was fourth on 307. It was generally agreed that Mitchell lost not only that Championship but, with it, all championships to come.

Of the great pre-war players, Herd had been best as runner-up on 305, Ray came next with a third-place finish on 306, Taylor was in 12th place on 316, Vardon in joint 14th on 318 and Braid in joint 20th on 320. The day of the Great Triumvirate, with 16 Open titles between them, was over.

The following year, when Duncan came fifth in an honourable defence of his title at St Andrews, the winner was Jock Hutchison, a Scotsman born in St Andrews in 1884 but by then a naturalized American. The famous old jug made its first transatlantic journey. Many, many more were to follow.

A sandy lie for George Duncan during the 1923 Open at Troon.
Below right *Ted Ray blasts his way out of the rough during the same championship.*

Jock Hutchison's Open victory in 1921 was the climax of a remarkable Championship in which he beat amateur Roger Wethered after a 36-hole play-off. No amateur had won since Harold Hilton in 1897 so Wethered's effort was particularly commendable.

In his first round of 72, Hutchison holed the 8th and 9th in a total of three strokes. He had a hole-in-one at the 8th and came within inches of another at the 9th. Then Wethered trod on his ball while searching for it and lost a penalty stroke in the third round. This, since he and Hutchison finished in a tie, has often been said to have lost him the title – which seems as ridiculous as to maintain that Hutchison gained it with his hole-in-one. If any particular shot could be said to have lost the Championship for Wethered it was surely his second shot to the 18th in the final round when his pitch after a fine drive finished short in the Valley of Sin, and, like many a man before him and since, he took three putts.

Although Arthur Havers won the Championship for Britain at Troon in 1923, golf had already entered an era in which it was dominated by one man, the greatest 'character' in the game between the wars – Walter Hagen. The extraordinary confidence of this flamboyant player is well illustrated by the story of how, on the eve of a play-off with Leo Diegel, Hagen was enjoying a few drinks into the small hours. Someone remarked to him that Diegel had gone upstairs a long time earlier, and Hagen replied: 'Yeah, but he ain't sleeping.'

Hagen reckoned to hit three or four rank bad shots in every round. He simply went out, hit them and promptly forgot about them. He was a masterly recovery player, and perhaps he and the Irish amateur, Jimmy Bruen, were the greatest experts of this period from

Jock Hutchison receives due acclaim following his Open win of 1921.
Below left Roger Wethered, who lost the play-off for the Open in 1921, is paired in the 1923 Amateur Championship with Francis Ouimet, the American amateur who had won the Open in 1913.

'impossible' situations.

He first came to Britain in 1920 and finished in comparative obscurity in Duncan's Championship at Deal, in joint 52nd place behind the winner in company with Mr T.D. Armour, a young Scottish amateur then aged 24 who was to turn professional, become a United States citizen and win the US Open in 1927.

Hagen came back for the next year's Open, Jock Hutchison's at St Andrews in 1921, and made a more pronounced impact, finishing seventh with six strokes between him and the winner, but doubtless able to reflect that if he had been allowed to swap Hutchison's final round of 70 for his own 77, he would have won by a shot.

He was back again the following year at Sandwich and this time he did win by a single shot. That made two successive American victories, an ominous portent, and with the exception of the Havers success at Troon in 1923 the next ten Opens were all won by Americans. It was a complete takeover. The pupils had become the masters with a vengeance, and the sons of the former masters had to sit at the feet of the former pupils and learn the game all over again.

It was Hagen's turn again at Hoylake in 1924 and then the title went to Jim Barnes, a tall, rangy Cornishman-turned-American who won at Prestwick in 1925. This Championship will always be remembered not so much as the one Barnes won but as the one Macdonald Smith lost.

Smith had long since left his native Carnoustie where he learned the fundamentals of his lovely swing, which was then trimmed and honed in America. When he arrived at Prestwick he was well set for an extraordinary battle. Barnes, who had won the US Open in 1921 and had tied second with Duncan, a shot behind Hagen, at Sandwich in 1922, streaked away from the field with an opening 70. The tables were turned on the following day when Smith shot a 69 against Barnes's 77 and led by two strokes at halfway. On the final day, Barnes had an 8 am start and, with Smith out late, this was the big Cornishman's chance. He missed it, and with a 79 against the Scotsman's 76 was now five behind. His 74 in the last round was good but surely not good enough, for it left Smith needing 78 to win and 79 to tie. Huge crowds arrived to see the Scotsman win, and in their determination to do so trampled poor Macdonald Smith into an 82 and fourth place on 303, three strokes adrift. So unwieldy were the Ayrshire hordes that the Championship, which had been played at Prestwick for the first 12 years of its existence, could never return there.

So continued the American domination of the oldest Open Championship in the world, and it was not until 1934 and Henry Cotton's brilliant victory at Sandwich that it was halted. If, with Hagen, the American challenge was already formidable, it became irresistible with the arrival on the scene of Bobby Jones, in the view of many the greatest golfer who ever lived.

Whether a golfer of one era can truly be compared with others of different eras is no easy matter. Ben Hogan, asked for his view, replied that it could not be done: 'A man can only beat the best players around in his time. Equipment improves, the condition of the courses gets better and competition increases all the time.'

All of Jones's three Open Championships were won in the days of the hickory shaft, in 1926, 1927, and in his Grand Slam year of 1930 when he achieved the entirely unparalleled feat of winning the Amateur and the Open Championships of both Britain and the US in the same year. At the end of it he retired

Congratulations for Open Champion Walter Hagen after the 1924 presentation ceremony.

altogether, in the words of Henry Longhurst, 'finally, completely, almost the only sporting figure to do so at his peak and with no second thoughts. He had indeed no more worlds to conquer and the rest must have been anti-climax. He was as near the perfect golfer as the game is likely to see, not merely in the perfection of his strokes but in the fact that his golfing manners, too, were perfect and every single soul who met him or watched him liked him.'

Jones played quickly and without fuss and, of course, without reference to the yardage charts which seem indispensable to the experts of today. He did observe a routine but it was a brief one and it never varied. Having looked towards the hole, he set the club behind the ball. His feet fell into position, very close together. One more glance down the line, one small waggle and away it went. Nothing more.

For years, it seemed, the golfing world had been waiting for Jones, ever since as a boy of 14 in 1916 he reached the third round of the US Amateur. He first came to Britain in 1921 but it was not until 1926 that he finally 'arrived'. By then he had won the US Amateur twice and the US Open once. He came for the Amateur at Muirfield but was defeated by Andrew Jamieson of Glasgow in the fifth round. In the subsequent Walker Cup match he got that out of his system by crushing Cyril Tolley, Britain's top amateur, by the huge margin of 12 and 11 and proceeded to Sunningdale for the qualifying rounds of the Open Championship to be played at Lytham and St Annes. At Sunningdale he played what is still talked about as the perfect round, when he scored 66. He holed one long putt for a three at the 5th, and found a bunker at the 13th but came out dead and got his three. Otherwise it was said to be the model, flawless round.

At Lytham, the Championship was still being played with one round on each of the first two days, followed by the final 36 holes on the final day, play then being restricted to those who were not more than 14 strokes behind the leader. After two days there were joint leaders. Jones with his two rounds of 72 and 'Wild Bill' Melhorn, with 70 and 74, were one shot clear of Hagen (68 and 77) and two ahead of Al Watrous. Jones and Watrous were paired together and Watrous turned the tables with a morning round of 69 against 73.

With five to play, Jones was still two behind but he got them back and they stood on the 17th tee level. Jones drove left into a flat,

Macdonald Smith leads his playing partner across the burn at Prestwick during his disastrous final round in 1925.

Bobby Jones gets his name on the Open trophy for the first time in 1926.

Crowds swarm around the scoreboard during the 1927 Open at St Andrews.
Far right *A hero's welcome for Bobby Jones on his return to New York after winning the British Open in 1930.*

shallow bunker in a wilderness of rough, Watrous into the prime position on the right from where he put his ball safely on the green but some distance from the flag. There followed what some regard as one of the greatest shots in golfing history, others as one of the great flukes of all time. Certainly Jones had been extremely fortunate that his ball had finished in the sand and not in the punishing, scruffy, sandy rough and that it was lying clean and far enough back from the face of the bunker to enable him to go for the green, although he had some pretty desperate stuff to carry.

He took a mashie-iron (about the equivalent of a modern No.5), took the ball clean and whipped it straight to the heart of the green, well inside the other. Poor Watrous took three putts and, with a four against five at the last hole, Jones won by two strokes.

He went home to win the American Open and returned to win again at St Andrews, where he had torn up his card a few years earlier because he found the course so difficult. But by 1927 it was very much a case of Jones versus the field. He led from the start at St Andrews and his total of 285 set a new low record for the Open. Almost unseen, but by no means unnoticed in ninth place came the ambitious young Henry Cotton, then 21.

The next two years belonged to the extravagant Walter Hagen then in 1930 Jones came back for the last time as a competitor to win the Grand Slam, or as it has been more prophetically called, the Impregnable Quadrilateral. Cotton moved up to eighth place. With Jones retired and Hagen past his best after four Open victories, there were still three American winners to come before the US grip was broken. They were Tommy Armour, Gene Sarazen and Densmore Shute.

Armour's victory came at Carnoustie and a gallant one it was as he came up from behind with a final round of 71, a great score over one of the sternest tests of golf in the world. His victory was the more meritorious in that he was suffering from the curious 'waggling disease' which so excruciatingly afflicted other players such as John de Forest and, later, Fred Daly. At his worst Daly needed up to 27 addresses before he could bring himself to hit the ball. These movements were neatly described by Leonard Crawley as like 'brushing a fly off the top of the ball'.

Armour at Carnoustie was not

Bobby Jones on his way to victory at St Andrews in 1927.
Far right *Tommy Armour (left) and Jim Barnes, both American winners of the Open.*

completely a victim. He could play his long shots confidently enough, with the minimum of preliminaries, but when it came to short pitches and sometimes to putting, he could not make up his mind to take the plunge. The strain on him must have been enormous but if he did not have mastery over his waggles he had it over himself, and that was what mattered.

Armour was deservedly champion but an even more memorable figure at Carnoustie was the small, smiling Argentinian, Jose Jurado. There was nothing hesitant about Jurado. He had a swing like greased lightning and was a great crowd pleaser with his dashing and pleasant manner. The Prince of Wales came to watch the Championship and had eyes for none but Jurado who was finally left with a 75 to win after Armour had returned his 71. It was a score well within his compass but leaving little margin. On the last tee he needed a four for 76 to tie and that required two full wooden club shots to clear the last bend of the meandering Barry Burn running across the face of the green. He hit a fine drive then, to the surprise of all, elected to play short of the water with an iron, pitched on in three and tried hard for his four but did not get it. Only when he had holed out was it realized that he had not known what he had to do. He must have been the only person who was unaware of this and it will forever be a mystery how it could possibly have been so.

The 1932 Championship was taken to Prince's, immediately adjacent to Royal St George's, for the first and only time and Gene Sarazen was a runaway winner with a best-ever score of 283. He had been second to Hagen just over the fence at Sandwich in 1928 and third to Armour at Carnoustie, so his victory did not come out of turn. The smiling, olive-skinned, gnome-like figure of Sarazen had become one of our most constant visitors and his attractive personality and attacking, almost casual outlook made him a most popular one. Bobby Jones, in describing Sarazen's game, wrote of him: 'It was Bang! Bang! Bang! all the time . . . he has for ever been the impatient, headstrong player who went for everything.'

He was born in the State of New York but was of pure Italian blood and began his golfing life as a caddie at Apawamis at the age of eight. He eluded the entire international early warning system and burst onto the American golfing scene in 1922 when he won the US Open, aged only 20, with a glorious final round

The Radio Times *recalls,
on a 1933 front cover,
Gene Sarazen's Open win
of the previous year.
Below Sarazen putting during
the 1932 Open.
Below right The 1928 Open
Championship as reported by
the* Illustrated Sporting
and Dramatic News.

of 68. If his win was surprising, he quickly provided evidence that it was no fluke when he proceeded to win the US PGA. His victory at Prince's meant that he had now won the three major championships of the world and, almost as soon as the US Masters was inaugurated, he joined the all-time élite by winning at Augusta in only its second year.

Sarazen first came to Britain in 1923 to play in the Open Championship at Troon where it had been taken for the first time. He came with his two American titles and failed to qualify. Like General MacArthur at a later date he said he would return – even if he had to swim across. There were no exempted players in those days.

Fifty years later he did. And of all things to do, he holed in one at the famous Postage Stamp with what he described as a 'punched 5-iron'. If ever a man should have handed his club back to his caddie and walked in, that was the moment! As somebody once said of Joe Davis in another game when he had

cleared every other ball off the table and was left with only the black: 'All he has to do now is go in off the chandelier and swallow the cue and we'll have seen everything.'

Still one Championship remained before the tide was to turn, at St Andrews in 1933. Home hopes were high, for Britain had just won the Ryder Cup (instituted in 1927) at Southport. But two Americans tied for the title, Densmore Shute and Craig Wood, and there were five Americans in the first six places. There was no doubting the quality of the two leading players, even though their play-off scores were nothing to write home about: Shute 149, Wood 154. Shute later won the US PGA title twice in a row (1936 and 1937), tied for the US Open in 1939 but lost the play-off, and was additionally runner-up in 1941. Wood won the US Open and Masters in 1941. These were all very great accomplishments, but in the winter of 1933–34 dynamic changes were in the air for those who could sense them.

In November 1929 the R & A announced: 'The Rules of Golf Committee have decided that steel shafts . . . are declared to conform with the requirements of the clause in the Rules of Golf on the form and make of golf clubs'. In this the R & A were following the USGA which had legalized steel shafts in 1924. So ended a dispute which had been going on since the first experimental steel-shafted clubs had emerged in the 1890s. The significance of the new ruling was profound, as profound as the arrival of the guttie ball had been in 1848, and that of the Haskell rubber core ball, around the turn of the century.

Steel shafts had been in limited use in America for some years, and a sizeable quantity had percolated to Britain. Many people had tried them and held various opinions on the subject.

It was rather like driving in the fast lane of a modern motorway at 80 mph or more when the limit is 70. Many people do it but no-one with any sense admits to it, unless to friends. All the Rules of Golf Committee did, in answer to public pressure, was to announce that they now regarded steel shafts as not offending against the rules.

The general conclusion was that the new clubs helped the weaker player to get perceptibly farther but had little effect on the hitting of the big men. The longer hitters certainly did not show the same enthusiasm as the shorter ones and some of them did not adopt steel for some time. Bobby Jones, for instance, won his four national championships in 1930 with wooden-shafted clubs. The mashie-iron with which he played his famous long bunker shot at the 17th hole at Royal Lytham and St Annes hangs on the wall of the Smoking Room and it certainly has a hickory shaft.

The average golfer was at once convinced that he liked a steel shaft in his woods but was not so easily converted about his irons, and most good players remained for some time strongly in favour of hickory shafted irons.

The mass production of steel shafts resulted in constant improvements in the ultimate product, but for some time after the arrival of 'matched sets' there was often a rogue club in the set which the player did not like. Modern technology has eliminated this and shafts are graded for 'whip' in a way that was not feasible in quantity with wood.

It also produced changes in technique in

that the same swing could be used for a far greater number of shots and, of course, resulted in many more clubs being used and carried. The authorities were in the end forced to place a limit on the number of clubs that could be carried and 14 was the number they settled on. Perhaps if they had made it 10 or even 12, the old art of half-shots would have been preserved and golf would have been a more attractive game to watch today.

In the Thirties the sand-wedge came out, and as well as causing a sensation at the time it had a lasting effect on the technique of the game, bringing the art of bunker play within the capabilities of anyone who could aim a reasonably precise blow at the ball. This led to the expression that the bunker shot could be bought at the pro's shop. The first models were heavy, egg-shaped, hollow-faced clubs, with a high back edge so that the club skidded and did not dig into the sand. The hollow face was soon declared illegal as it was ruled that it hit the ball twice. The form and the principle of the club

have remained the same. The method has been refined in that the club in the hands of the expert is made to skid in a shallow arc under the ball with no great force needed, whereas in the days of Walter Hagen – who was said to aim for a bunker at a difficult green – the 'explosion' shot was the vogue. It required less touch but Hagen was a master at getting the ball out near the pin.

It was during the late autumn of 1930 that millionaire Clifford Roberts went to Atlanta to suggest to Bobby Jones that he should join him in organizing a club and building a golf course at nearby Augusta. Jones had but recently announced his retirement from competitive golf at the early age of 28 after achieving his unique Grand Slam.

The project appealed to Jones who, with his vast experience and brilliant mind, chose Dr Alister MacKenzie as the architect to design the course with him, the whole concept to be set up on a national basis. Not the most inconsiderable factor in their compatibility was that they were both 'extravagant admirers' of the Old Course at St Andrews and both desired to simulate seaside conditions insofar as the differences in turf and terrain would allow. MacKenzie's creed as a golf course architect was that he tried to build courses for the 'most enjoyment for the greatest number' and this concided completely with Jones's own view.

As far as possible they sought to present to each golfer an interesting problem which would test him without being so impossibly difficult that he would have little chance of success. From the standpoint of the inexpert player there is nothing so completely disheartening as being confronted by a carry which is beyond his best effort and which offers no alternative route. There must be a way round for those unwilling or unable to attempt the carry and there must be definite reward awaiting the man who makes it. Without the alternative route it is unfair, and without the reward is meaningless.

Possibly the dearth of bunkers on the course is the feature most commented upon by visitors. There are some which could be dispensed with, except that they are there to protect players from more dire consequences. The over-riding requirement was that the course should be within the capacity of the average golfer.

Augusta was designed to offer a golf course and a retreat to men of 'some means' who were devoted to the game. It would also be a place of such luxury that they would come from all over the United States to play with kindred spirits. This policy has never changed. The retreat was also to be a place of natural beauty, adorned with flowering shrubs and rare trees and the course a place of peace and

Bobby Jones's personal book plate.
Below left *Crowds watch Bobby Jones in action during his third US Open victory at Winged Foot in 1929.*
Below *Bobby Jones (right) with Gene Sarazen at the US Open of 1923.*

recreation as well as a superb golf course.

In due course there came the suggestion that Augusta should try to attract the US Open Championship, but the main opposing reason was that if played so far south, the event would have to be held in early spring instead of the customary month of June or early July. Clifford Roberts then came up with the idea of staging a tournament of their own, building it around the role of Jones as host on his one annual appearance in competition. As president of the club it was also to be his privilege to invite those whom he considered likely to grace the tournament by reason of past accomplishments, their present stature, their promise or even his own feelings of friendship for them. It took no time at all for them to decide that this system was much too lax and caused embarrassment, and that rigid qualification requirements must be set and adhered to. Players nevertheless had to be invited to take part, and this characteristic has always been retained.

The first tournament was called the Augusta Invitation Tournament and was played in 1934, less than four years after the project was first mooted. The first winner was Horton Smith who beat Craig Wood by one stroke with a total of 284. The event gained immediate favour. The Press as much as anyone dubbed it 'The Masters' and so it has become known. The club remains as 'exclusive' as ever, perhaps a little too much so in these days, but there is no doubting the peculiar demands on the skill and the minds and nerves of everyone who seeks to conquer the course.

The plaque at Augusta commemorating Gene Sarazen's historic shot.
Below right Horton Smith, winner of the first US Masters.
Bottom Byron Nelson playing in the Ryder Cup at Southport in 1937, the year of his first US Masters victory.

In the 1933 Open Henry Cotton had been one of five players sharing seventh place behind the American quintet at St Andrews in company, be it noted, with Alf Padgham and Reg Whitcombe, all three of them only three shots adrift and all destined to emblazon their names on the trophy in the five years to follow – once Cotton had broken the ten long years of American domination.

Cotton had gone to the United States at a time when he could barely afford it to compete with the best American players and to address himself intelligently to learning their secrets. More than any man before or since he had trained himself mentally and physically and had spent so long practising his short game that, as he said, it was easier for him to continue in a crouched position than to try and stand upright. He had outrightly declared his intention to win the Open Championship, to reach the highest pinnacles of his profession, and he applied himself intensely, unremittingly and often controversially to the achievement of these lofty ambitions.

To their acquisition he brought not only all the energy and determinaton with which Nature had endowed him but also a darting and acute mind, an enjoyment of the limelight and a disregard of public opinion. More than any golfer since the days of Harry Vardon, and now, to a vastly wider public, he became a household name. Whether as a golfer, as a forthright and amusing speaker, as an entertaining writer and even on the music-hall stage, he compelled attention. He had striven long and hard and had waited as patiently as he could for the culmination of all his efforts. When it came at Sandwich in 1934, it was nothing short of sensational and, in its knock-on effect, something like Roger Bannister's four-minute mile. Everybody began to do it. The next five winners of the Open were all British.

It is true that the tide of the American invasion was on the ebb and few of them were at Sandwich in 1934. Lest this sound uncharitable, let it be said that although this will forever be remembered as Cotton's year, the true and complete consummation of his powers did not come until three years later. Then, in perhaps the fiercest conditions under which the Open had ever been played, he routed the full array of the victorious American Ryder Cup team at Carnoustie. That was his second

Henry Cotton (right) with his brother at the Boys' Championship of 1921.

Henry Cotton on the tee and (below) on the green during the Open of 1934 in which he turned the tide of American domination.

*Alf Perry, Open
Champion in 1935.*

triumph and he was to complete his hat-trick at
Muirfield in 1948, 11 years later when the war
was over.

Sandwich, however, was beyond
question the most sensational. He had scored a
66 in one of the qualifying rounds and then in
the real thing he began with a 67. His 65 in the
second round was stunning and his total of 132
for a halfway lead of eight strokes was
unheard-of stuff. The Dunlop 65 ball was named
to commemorate the feat and is still around
today, more than fifty years later.

The morning of the last day was
blustery, with squalls of rain and hail, and in
such conditions Cotton's round of 72 was
admirably adequate. His position was more
secure than ever and it remained only for him to
cruise home as he pleased. But there's many a
slip twixt the cup and the lips. They say that he
ate something that disagreed with him for lunch
and certainly he looked pale and drawn when he
appeared on the 1st tee for his final round.

Many began to remember that even the
great Bobby Jones used to suffer so badly from
stomach nerves that he was either unable to eat
at all or, if he did, was immediately sick.
Whatever had happened to him, Cotton
certainly kept everyone on tenterhooks for hours
and the anguish was in no way eased when it
became possible that some of the greens might
become flooded.

*Alf Padgham, the third
British Open Champion in
succession when he won in
1936.*

He began with a scrambled five at the
1st and ran up sixes at the 5th and the 7th to be
out in 40, with the sterner half to come. It is
held at Sandwich that anyone who is to come
home in reasonable figures must secure three
fours to begin with. Cotton took three fives.
Now seven over fours, he had three long holes
to face. He really was up against it now. If this
sort of thing did not stop soon, and there
seemed no reason why it should, we were about
to witness the most appalling 'blow-up' in
recorded history.

However, stop it did, at the very next
hole, which happened to be the 'unlucky' 13th,
straight out to Prince's clubhouse. He could not
get up in two but he pitched beautifully and
holed the putt for a four. The next two holes
have ruined many a card, first the long 14th or
Suez Canal, with trouble everywhere, then the
15th with its cross bunkers and severely
undulating green, and the hole cut on that tiny
plateau at the back – somewhat reminiscent of
the eccentric 16th green at North Berwick. Any

golf-course architect designing it today would be locked up! Cotton got splendid fours at both and now, barring accidents, he was surely home and dry. The agony was over, the cup was his at last; but better, much, much better was still to come.

The following year at Muirfield, that fairest and noblest of all championship links, came another new British champion, the jaunty, fearless Alf Perry. It is true that he had figured reasonably prominently in a few recent championships but he had never seriously looked like winning before, nor did he ever again, although to be fair to him he finished joint third in Dick Burton's year of 1939. He had also reached the final of the News of the World in 1932, only to be heavily beaten by Cotton.

In those now far-off days there were no scoreboards dotted around the course to keep spectators informed, only the names of the three or so leaders chalked on a blackboard. Prize-money totalled £500, with £100 to the winner.

Although Cotton had opened brilliantly with a 68 in defence of his title, he slipped from close contention as Perry improved until, when he holed out at the short 16th Perry required a six and a five to win. At the 17th tee the fingers on his right hand hung loosely from the club and he seemed to have a rather 'agricultural', scythe-like action. However the ball went off like a rocket and he cheerfully whacked another wooden club shot to the heart of the green. He did the same again at the 18th and, if he secretly had any fear of winning, he never gave the slightest sign that this was so.

The following year, 1936, was unquestionably Alf Padgham's year. He won everything, including the Open at Hoylake. He was in advance of his time in holding his arms well away from his body when putting. He stood very upright, some way from the ball, and hit it rather as if he were playing a short chip from off the green. Whatever the reason, his ball seemed to hug the turf more than most and continued to roll smoothly until it toppled into the hole when so often it looked as if it would never get there. It would, however, be a complete injustice to a great golfer to suggest that he was little more than a magnificent putter. He was completely and impressively armed at all points, including an unbelievably serene temperament. They said latterly of James Braid that nobody could be as wise as Braid looked and it would be equally true to say of Padgham that nobody could possibly be as placid as

Padgham appeared.

If his putting was a little unusual, the rest of his game was entirely orthodox and the sleepy power of his driving, and particularly his long iron shots up to the flag, was something to savour and to marvel at. His backswing was short, he never seemed to hit hard to the ball yet it flew off with a sharp crack and he was among the longest hitters of his day.

In the end, it was a duel between Padgham and Jimmy Adams, a Scotsman born and bred in Troon, with a long flowing swing and, at the time, professional at Romford. Eventually, Padgham had four to tie, and three to win. His high pitch finished some fifteen feet from the hole and, apparently as casual as ever, he holed it for victory. Adams, another with a lovely putting touch, finished runner-up as he did again at Sandwich two years later.

The next two Championships were marred by dreadful weather, first at Carnoustie where Cotton won with a marvellous final round of 71, played in appalling conditions of wind and rain. All through a worrying, drenching afternoon it was touch-and-go whether the men with the squeegees could keep the greens clear enough to allow play to be

Henry Cotton, the national hero.

The Whitcombe brothers.
Left to right: Reg, Ernest
and Charles.

completed. Reg Whitcombe finished second, two strokes behind Cotton but he was to win at Sandwich the following year and at last get the name of a Whitcombe onto the trophy for himself and his brothers who had done so much for British golf.

For the first two days at Sandwich in 1938 the weather was positively benign, the skylarks were trilling and the scoring was hot. Then in the night there rose a mighty storm and the spectacle that awaited the early arrivals at the course was one of utter devastation. Flags had been ripped to tatters, tents blown down and it was only a matter of time before the huge exhibition tent was torn apart and its merchandise scattered all over the place. And still the wind blew, harder than ever. An illustration of its strength was that Padgham drove the 11th and holed for two. Not so happy was the mighty Cyril Tolley who hit a full drive followed by a 1-iron at the 14th and watched helplessly as his ball soared far over the Canal, only to be blown back into the water.

Jimmy Adams, paired with Whitcombe, was again in the thick of the action.

Whitcombe led by two strokes at the start of the final round but took four putts on the 1st green and his lead vanished. Similar instances of prodigality took place on either side as they fought their way round until Whitcombe finally settled it with a terrific four at the 17th – two tremendous shots into the teeth of the gale, a long run-up and a brave putt holed. Now he could afford a careful five at the 18th and won by two strokes.

One last thrill remained. Cotton went out late with a 71 to win. Among other brilliant thrusts, he drove the second (370 yd/338m) for a three, was out in 35 and almost unbelievably began for home with 4, 3, 3. In the end, he had to settle for a 74 and third place but his 74 was the best of a wild afternoon in which only seven of the 36 starters could beat 80.

Now we go to St Andrews again for the 1939 Championship and we come first to the winner, Richard Burton, a tall lean man standing well over six feet. He had a pronounced flail at the top of a flowing swing which sent the ball a very long way, though not always in the desired direction. Henry Cotton said of him: 'I think he

Jimmy Bruen, a force to be reckoned with at St Andrews in 1939.

revelled in being called a long driver, and in order not to let down his public he tried to make every tee shot an enormous one, and so made scoring difficult for himself.'

The name on everybody's lips at St Andrews was, however, that of the young Irish amateur, Jimmy Bruen, a serious contender beforehand and the more so when he had led the qualifiers with 69 over each of the Old and New courses. Bruen had a swing all of his own. Nothing like it had ever been seen before. There was the famous loop at the top which saw the club pointing at right-angles to the line of flight instead of at the target and which, since it never stopped and did not, like everyone else, have to set off in a reciprocal direction no matter how brief the turn-about, gave him enormous speed at impact and made him one of the longest hitters the game has ever seen. This was certainly the case from the rough, from which he achieved prodigious distances.

Many people thought that Bruen might well win and, when he came off the last green with a 77 in his third round, Burton's first words were: 'What has Bruen done?' On being

told 75, his comment was: 'Thank God for that!' At the start of the third round, Burton with scores of 70 and 72 had held a five-stroke lead over Bruen (72 and 75) but the anxious inquiry showed that Burton felt the Irish lad was capable of almost anything and was the only man he genuinely feared. Bruen in fact finished joint 13th in the distinguished company of Henry Cotton and Jimmy Adams.

Burton had his ups and downs en route to a final 71 but the shot that will stay with all who saw it was the nonchalant, almost supercilious, flick of the wrists with the most lofted club in his bag – a wide-soled blaster type of niblick – which deposited his ball some five yards behind the stick at the 18th. He had not flinched in his choice of club after an enormous drive almost into the Valley of Sin for that fateful shot, and he did not hesitate over the putt. With scarcely more than a glance at the line, he rolled it in. He threw his putter to his caddie when the ball was only halfway there, so confident was he that he had holed it! His victory was a fitting curtain to 20 years of championship golf between the wars.

Ernest Holderness during the Amateur Championship of 1924.

In the twenty-five years or so leading up to the First World War it was not uncommon for amateurs to figure prominently in the Open Championship and not too uncommon for one of them to win it. A small number of them continued to hold their own with the professionals even after the famous triumvirate arrived in the persons of Taylor, Vardon and Braid. The last of them to win the title was Harold Hilton who intruded at Hoylake in 1897 after Taylor had won twice and Vardon once. It must be remembered, however, that numbers were small and that in no year had the total entry reached a hundred in number.

The war made a clean sweep of the top amateurs in the golfing sense and into the arena marched a new trio, widely different in temperament and method but forever to be bracketed together. They were Roger Wethered, Cyril Tolley and Sir Ernest Holderness. Wethered takes pride of place in the group since he very nearly succeeded in turning back the clock in the 1921 Open, losing in a play-off against Jock Hutchison at St Andrews. The new heroes won four out of the first five Amateur Championships after the war. In physical stature and presence Tolley took the eye, his driving being majestic; Wethered's driving was never quite on a par with his iron play while Holderness, without the power of the other two, was safe and reliable.

When Bob Gardner reached the final in 1920, the first Championship after the war, only the rather unfriendly, black-cigar-smoking Walter Travis, a deadly putter, had ever won the trophy for America (1904) since it started in 1885. Gardner, an all-round athlete who had held the world pole-vaulting record, was beaten only at the 37th by Tolley. Six years later Jesse Sweetser took the title to America for a second time. Sweetser had won the American Amateur in 1922 and was a popular and much-respected figure on both sides of the Atlantic. His win for America was followed after a four-year interval by Bobby Jones in his Grand Slam year of 1930.

The victorious years of Tolley, Wethered and Holderness were followed by a win for Robert Harris. He had twice before reached the final where he had fallen first to Hilton, then to Wethered. Harris made the third time pay for all when, in 1925, he won at Westward Ho! by 13 and 12 – the largest winning margin to that date. His record was not

Top Roger Wethered and Cyril Tolley (below) in action on the tee at Prestwick in 1922.
Bottom Bob Gardner, who came near to taking the Amateur Championship back to the United States in 1920.
Facing page Jesse Sweetser, American winner of the Amateur Championship in 1926.
Below Robert Harris, who won the 1925 Amateur Champtionship by an impressive margin against the unfortunate Kenneth Fradgley.

surpassed until nine years later. Then in sensational fashion Lawson Little won at Prestwick by 14 and 13. Little won again in 1935 and assured himself of an undying place in history by winning the American Amateur as well in both years before turning professional and winning the American Open in 1940, after a play-off with Gene Sarazen.

Lawson Little was an exceptional golfer and an intimidating, even alarming adversary. The power of his rather shut-faced swing was immense, he was broad-shouldered and enormously strong, capable, as Bernard Darwin wrote of him, 'of a daunting pugnacity of expression'; and with it all, he was possessed of the silken touch of so many very strong men on and around the greens.

His first victory, at Prestwick, set a two-pronged record that may stand for all time. Round in 66 against James Wallace in the morning, he was 12 up at lunch and the starting-time for the second round was advanced to enable him to catch the boat for home. (There was no jet-plane travel in those days.) He had eight threes in the morning and four more in the five holes he required for victory after lunch. So there he was with 12 threes in 23 holes and winner by a record margin – by twenty past two in the afternoon!

But if he had things all his own way at Prestwick, it was a very different matter at Royal Lytham when he returned to defend his trophy the following year. From the start he allowed himself to be harried by players he would have swept aside the year before but, with the great golfer's ability to play the really brilliant shot when most needed, he won through and it was generally expected that in the final he would run away from his opponent, Dr William Tweddell, now that he had room to manoeuvre over 36 holes. Tweddell had won the title eight years earlier, and although his method was far from orthodox he was nothing if not a fighter. Although cruelly outdriven, he cheerfully clung to his man and took him all the way to the 36th green. It was one of the most 'heroic performances ever seen but this time David did not beat Goliath. Little thus became the first champion successfully to defend his title since Harold Hilton at the turn of the century.

In 1933 the Hon. Michael Scott became, and remains, the oldest winner at the age of 54, and just before him was John de Forest, who had also reached the final in 1931. De Forest's

The Hon Michael Scott who won the Amateur Championship in 1933 at the age of 54.

two finals will be remembered for the unfortunate golfing malady under which he laboured. Only those who have suffered from this ridiculous ailment, whereby the player gets stuck and gazes fixedly at the ball, motionless as though in a trance and quite unable to move the club. If it was tiresome for the watchers, just think of the effects on the player himself, and on his opponent.

Little was followed by one of the most stylish players ever to win the Amateur, Hector Thomson. Thomson's second shot to the 36th hole at St Andrews, when one up, will forever be remembered by the many thousands who watched as he almost holed it to beat a dangerous Australian challenger in Jim Ferrier by two holes. There was nothing left for Ferrier to do, with his own ball on the back of the green, but to walk forward and shake the new champion by the hand.

Incidentally, it was in that year, 1936, that Bobby Locke came to Britain for the first time, trailing clouds of glory from a scintillating record in his native South Africa. He was beaten by Morty Dykes before he got started but soon showed what he was made of by finishing as the leading amateur, in joint eighth position, in the ensuing Open at Hoylake. He repeated that performance the following year but was beaten again in an early round of the Amateur, this time by Gordon Peters.

Following Hector Thomson's classic victory at St Andrews, the next two Amateurs went to Americans in the persons of Robert Sweeney and the immensely popular Charlie Yates. Alex Kyle, a Borders Scot long settled in Yorkshire, won in 1939 but just as the Americans had taken over the Open for ten successive years from 1924, so they were beginning to take over the Amateur. Including Lawson Little's double, in the six years until the outbreak of the Second World War four out of six winners were Americans.

No account of amateur golf between the wars would be complete without reference to Jack McLean of Scotland and Eric Fiddian of England. Both were Walker Cup players, and McLean won the Scottish Amateur three years in a row in the Thirties and also came very close to winning the American Amateur in 1936 but was beaten by a long putt at the 37th hole by Johnny Fischer after a stymie had robbed him of victory; Fiddian, beaten by de Forest in the final of the 1932 Amateur, won the English Amateur that

year. The two met in the final of the Irish Open Amateur championship in 1933 when Fiddian accomplished the extraordinary feat of twice

William Tweddell is presented with the Amateur Championship trophy by the captain of the Royal Liverpool Golf Club at Hoylake in 1927.

holing-in-one, once in the morning and once in the afternoon. It did him no good, though, for McLean beat him by 3 and 2. As an interesting comparison, Vardon and Hagen only ever had one hole-in-one apiece.

67

The scorer's tent at the 1922 Ladies' Championship at Prince's Sandwich, which was won by Joyce Wethered. Below Joyce Wethered at St Andrews in 1929.

When hostilities ceased in Europe, one player dominated women's golf. She was Cecil Leitch, who had made her first impact on the game in 1908 at St Andrews and in 1914 had carried off the British Open, the English and the French Open Championships.

In 1919 everything was ready for the British Open to be resumed when a railway strike upset the arrangements. The English Championship was held that year, however, and at St Annes Miss Leitch clearly showed that the pre-war queen had no intention of being usurped, crushing Mrs Temple Dobell, her opponent in the final, by 10 and 8.. She was only slightly more merciful on Miss Molly Griffiths when she was at last able to defend her British title at Newcastle, Co. Down in 1920. Strong, energetic and immensely vital, she was a natural leader and it seemed she would go on winning titles as long as she wanted.

Then, as suddenly and unexpectedly as Miss Leitch herself had appeared there arrived an even greater player who was to dominate her realm as Bobby Jones did his at a later date. It happened at Sheringham, where Miss Leitch arrived to defend her English title a month after her triumph in the British; surely she would make it three in a row, or so everyone supposed.

The prelude to the English was an 18-hole qualifying round and no-one took the slightest notice of the occupant of 25th place, a tall, slender, pallid young lady who had come to Sheringham as companion to Miss Griffiths, with no thoughts of setting the whole golfing world ablaze. Thus, modestly and

unobtrusively, arrived Joyce Wethered.

She left a trail of awestruck opponents behind her as she advanced to the final, Miss Leitch doing the same in the other half of the draw. And what a contrast they made. Miss Leitch, who habitually took charge on the 1st tee as naturally as she drew breath, was a dominating figure. Her swing was flat, she used a palm grip with the right hand markedly under the shaft and looked the very embodiment of dash and power, which indeed she was. Miss Wethered, tall, slim and fragile, was by nature shy and retiring. People now crowded forward to stare at this elegant, wraith-like being who had come among them as from another planet to see if she was really true. But she shunned the public gaze as much as she could, vanishing when her matches were over to be seen no more

Cecil Leitch at Sheringham in 1920.

until the starter called her name for the next round. She would come to the 1st tee, smile charmingly to her opponent, and then completely lose herself in a cocoon of concentration. In the graphic words of a later champion, Enid Wilson, who knew her well: 'Her seeming remoteness from all the stress and strain that trouble ordinary people bewildered her opponents, her indifference to what they did became positively nightmarish.'

Joyce Wethered had become a student of the game largely because of her brother, Roger, and must have theorized on the composition of the golf swing in a manner which no other woman had ever done before. Playing with her talented brother and his friends developed her game quickly and made her impervious to superior physical power. That and an obviously inherited natural talent and balance gave her the belief that the way to play golf was to swing as perfectly as she could, to play the game her way and the result would take care of itself. It certainly produced the goods and so captivated Bobby Jones when he played with her that he declared her to be the finest woman golfer he had ever seen or was ever likely to see.

Miss Wethered won that first encounter in 1920 and the two of them so captured the public imagination that any meeting of the pair became an event of national importance which thousands turned out to watch.

When Miss Wethered decided she had done all she wanted to do and called it a day in 1924, she was still only 24. In the brief span of years since her advent in 1920, she had captured three British titles and won the English five years in a row. She continued to give her adoring public a glimpse of herself by playing in the Worplesdon Mixed Foursomes and ran up the almost incredible record of eight victories, with seven different partners. She came back in 1929 when she could not resist the lure of St Andrews and in the final of the British Championship beat Glenna Collett, easily the best and most powerful golfer on the other side of the Atlantic. When Miss Leitch retired it was also with four British victories and two English in her 15 years. Between them they had raised the standing and the standard of women's golf. They had truly been in a class all by themselves but a satisfactory number of young ones were coming along to take their place.

Miss Collett reached the final again the following year where she was attended to by

Joyce Wethered, unbeatable in the early 1920s.
Left An impressive mixed foursome about to begin a challenge match in the United States in 1935. Left to right: Gene Sarazen, Joyce Wethered, Glenna Collett and Johnny Dawson.

The French flag flies proudly over the final green at Hunstanton in 1928. Below Large crowds follow Pam Barton during the Ladies' Championship at Southport in 1936. Far right Pam Barton gives advice to an RAF colleague in 1943.

Diana Fishwick, just 19, twice winner of the Girls' Championship, who played with the coolness of a veteran in her victory by 4 and 3.

The Ladies' Golf Union had been looking anxiously to the West all this time but it turned out that they should have been looking in the other direction for, just as Arnaud Massy of France had been the first foreigner to win the Open Championship, in 1907, so France produced the next two winners of the British Ladies' Championship. They were Miss Thion de la Chaume in 1927, followed by Miss Nanette Le Blan. Diana Fishwick triumphed in 1930 and then came the first of Miss Wilson's three successive victories.

Miss Wilson was followed by Mrs Andrew Holm, who took the trophy to Scotland where it had not been since 1911. She took it back there again in 1938 after the exciting arrival in the winner's enclosure of the young, fresh-faced Pam Barton who had been runner-up to Mrs Holm in 1934 and to Wanda Morgan in 1935.

'Wee' Jessie Anderson from Perth took the title from Miss Barton in 1937 and was to put herself among the all-time greats by winning two more times after the war as Mrs George Valentine, as well as capturing six Scottish championships and a host of other honours too numerous to mention. Pam Barton won again in 1939, the last British Open before the outbreak of war, and there is no saying how far she might have gone and how many titles she might have gained had she not tragically been killed in a flying accident while serving with the Women's Auxiliary Air Force. She was buried with military honours at Manston, Kent in 1943.

Wanda Morgan and Enid Wilson (right), two leading ladies in the 1930s.

British golfer Jack Neville
splashes out of the Swilcan
burn during the first Walker
Cup match in the UK at St
Andrews in 1923.

*British golfer Jack Neville
splashes out of the Swilcan
burn during the first Walker
Cup match in the UK at St
Andrews in 1923.*

he great international matches
which we now take for granted
were all born and grew up
between the wars. The main
ones are, of course, those
between the Americans and teams drawn from
the golfers of Great Britain and Ireland.

Walker Cup
The first amateur match between Great Britain
and Ireland and the USA was played at Hoylake,
home of the great innovators, in 1921, which
America won by nine matches to three. The
Amateur Championship was being played at
Hoylake that year. Mr G.H. Walker of the
United States thereupon presented a Cup to be
known as 'The United States Golf Association
Challenge Trophy' but always popularly known
as the 'Walker Cup'.

The first official match took place at
Long Island in August 1922, and was won 8-4
by America. The next match was held at St
Andrews in 1923 where the home side lost again
but only by the odd match, 6½–5½. At Garden
City, New York in 1924 America won again, by
9–3, and it was agreed that the event would
thereafter be played every two years, alternately
in each country.

The only time Britain failed to win a
single match was at Pine Valley in 1936 but the
team avoided a whitewash by halving three of
the 12 matches. In 1938 the great day came at
last at St Andrews when the British triumphed
7-4 and took the Walker Cup for the first time
(and the last until 1971).

*The British Walker Cup
team of 1930 which lost to
Bobby Jones and his
American colleagues.
Back, left to right: W.
Campbell, R. Hartley,
J.A. Stout, J.N. Smith.
Seated: T.A. Torrance,
C.J. Tolley, R.H.
Wethered, Sir E.
Holderness.*

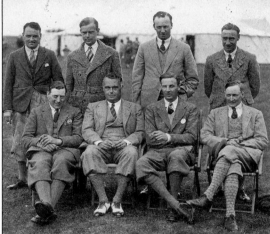

Ryder Cup
The first engagement between the professionals
of Great Britain and Ireland and the United
States took place at Gleneagles in 1921 and was
won 10½–4½ by the home side who came
precious near to inflicting a complete whitewash
at Wentworth in 1926. Bill Melhorn beat Archie
Compston by one hole and Emmett French
halved with Ernest Whitcombe to make the
result 13½–1½ for Great Britain and Ireland.

The famous Cup was presented by Mr
Samuel Ryder, a seedsman of St Albans, and
was first competed for in 1927 at Worcester,
Mass. In 1929 the original conditions were
tightened to confine the British team to British-
born professionals resident in Great Britain, and
the American team to American-born
professionals who were resident in the United

*Bobby Jones receives the
congratulations of Roger
Wethered after the
American team had won the
Walker Cup in 1930, the
year of Bobby Jones's
Grand Slam.*

States in the year of the match (Scots-born Tommy Armour had been included in the American team in 1926). The contest, like the Walker Cup, takes place in alternate years, each country being visited in turn. Alterations in the format of play have been made from time to time but the only major change to the conditions came in 1979 when the British team was extended to include European players. At the outbreak of the Second World War, America led by four matches to two.

Curtis Cup

In the women's game the Vagliano Cup was presented in 1931 by a kind Frenchman of that name for annual competition between Britain and France. Then in 1932 Miss Margaret and Miss Harriot Curtis of Boston, Mass., presented the Curtis Cup for biennial competition between teams from the United States of America and Great Britain and Ireland. Up to that time no American lady in the long history of the British Ladies' Championship had succeeded in winning and only Glenna Collett (twice) had ever reached the final.

Britain's record in the Curtis Cup match is, however, as dismal as that of the men, amateur and professional, in their jousts with the USA. In the four years of competition up to the Second World War the best that Britain's ladies could achieve was a symmetrical tie in 1936, each team gaining 1½ points in the foursomes and 3 points in the singles.

Home International Matches

It was away back in 1902 that the Scotland v

Abe Mitchell drives from the first tee at Wentworth during the first match between the professionals of Britain and the United States in 1926.

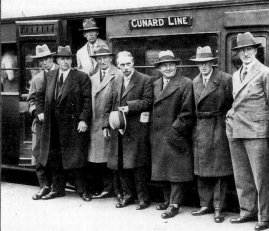

Members of the Ryder Cup team about to leave for the United States in 1927. Left to right: Archie Compston, Ted Ray, George Duncan, F. Robson, Sam Ryder, George Gadd, Charles Whitcombe and Arthur Havers.

Walter Hagen points out the sights of London to his Ryder Cup colleagues from the roof of the Savoy Hotel in 1929. Left to right: Jim Turnesa, Leo Diegel, Al Espinosa, Horton Smith, Walter Hagen, Al Watrous.
Far left Dorothy Chambers (left), the English captain, and Glenna Collett Vare, captain of the American team, share the presentation ceremony after the first Curtis Cup to be tied in 1936.

Markers defy the elements during the 1936 Curtis Cup match at Gleneagles.

England match was first played, at Hoylake, and it went on for a number of years as a prelude to the Amateur Championship until it was abandoned in 1913 because, in the words of Englishman Bernard Darwin, 'the Scotsmen were too good and won too often'. Attempts to restart it never came to much but finally in 1932 the various Unions took charge, incorporated Ireland and Wales, and the series as we know it today began.

Enthusiasm was rekindled, rivalry was intense and large crowds turned up to watch. All this has waned again, the players and officials remain as keen as mustard but the main value of the series appears to be its opportunities for young men to show their credentials for higher honours, opportunities perhaps denied them in the championships by reasons of bad luck or a bad draw or an inferior opponent who 'goes mad' for one round. Sports editors of the various newspapers and other branches of the media, obsessed with the vast amounts of cash being played for by the professionals all over the world, must take part of the blame. But then, as Nigel Dennis put it: 'One is always excited by descriptions of money changing hands. It's much more fundamental than sex.'

PART THREE

THE POSTWAR YEARS,
1946–1959

It was a brilliantly simple idea, as the best ideas often are. Why not have a team competition open to every golfing nation in the world? That would do something to reunite a world that had recently been shattered by the Second World War. And so it came about, a competition 'for the furtherance of better understanding among the nations of the world through the medium of international golf competition'.

It was the idea of John Jay Hopkins, an American industrialist with big-business interests in Canada. For obvious reasons he named it the Canada Cup. The format was for each competing nation to enter two men and the winner would be the team with the lowest combined total for 72 holes of stroke-play.

Ben Hogan is watched by partner Sam Snead during the Canada Cup at Wentworth in 1956.

Few competitions in the immediate post-war period began other than precariously and this was no exception. The world had hardly recovered from the war. Money was scarce, air travel was in its infancy. In Britain rationing had only just ended. The first steps the Canada Cup took in 1953 were indeed trembling ones. It was staged over 36 holes at a course just outside Montreal and eight nations were represented. Yet it caught the imagination of the public to such an extent that the next year, again played over 36 holes, more than three times as many countries competed.

The Canada Cup fell into good hands when Fred Corcoran, an Irish American, took it over in 1954. Corcoran was steeped in golf. He had been a caddie before starting to manage players, both men and women. Among those in his stable were Sam Snead and Babe Zaharias. Corcoran was a born entrepreneur. In 1936 he had become the first full-time director of the USPGA tour at a salary of $75 a week and $35 a week for expenses. In ten years he trebled the number of events on the tour and raised prize-money to $750,000.

Corcoran soon realized the potential of the Canada Cup. He began moving it around the world, thereby promoting both it and golf. In its first two decades it was held in places as far apart as Hawaii, England, Japan, France, Singapore, Venezuela and Australia.

As luck would have it (and he was Irish, remember) a few of the earliest Canada Cups were outstandingly successful and this excitement cemented the event into the imagination of the public. For example, when it

was held at Wentworth in 1956 Ben Hogan, who was then well past 40, and Sam Snead won the team event for the US and Hogan took the individual title as well. It was the last time that Hogan played in Britain and thousands tramped around the Burma Road to pay their respects to the man who had won the US Masters, US Open and the Open in four stunning months in 1953.

It was of this year's Canada Cup that the great golfing journalist Bernard Darwin was moved to write: '. . . In point of cosmopolitan character nothing that has gone before can quite compare with the Canada Cup. It is such a competition as might have been played, had golf then been invented, under the shadow of the Tower of Babel. Never have so many players assembled from so many different countries. The

champions of diverse lands have played in our Open championships but not so many as this time at Wentworth, and moreover they have played as individuals whereas now they are members of their countries' teams. That fact gives an added poignancy. It seems to combine in some degree the thrills of match and medal . . .'

In 1957, in Japan, Torakichi (Pete) Nakamura and Koichi Ono delighted the home crowd to take the team event. Nakamura won the individual trophy. There was as much enthusiasm at Portmarnock, Ireland, in 1960. It is estimated that 60,000 spectators attended the famous course outside Dublin to see if Ireland could repeat their famous victory of two years earlier in Mexico City. They could not.

Despite their enormous depth of talent

*Bobby Jones, a welcome
visitor to Chicago in 1928.*

Postcards and cigarette cards portraying golf as very much a way of life.

Above More golf themes for magazine covers in the Twenties.
Right Worldwide golfing holidays were vigorously promoted in the years between the wars.

A Norman Rockwell cover for The Saturday Evening Post.

Far left Golf literature for the serious enthusiast, and (below) a wide range of lighter reading.

Right *A golf scene created by Carlton Ware and used on a wide range of products.*
Below *Two famous figures who competed for space in the professional's shop.*
Below right *Silver hatpins and other golf-associated silverware.*
Bottom right *Golfing pairs – Blackheath golfers at the back and, in front, two Austrian figures from the 1920s.*

and although they have won more often than any other country, the US have not dominated the event. Argentina, Australia, Japan, Ireland, South Africa, Canada, Taiwan and Spain (in part thanks to a prodigy named Seve Ballesteros) have all taken the team event at some time or another. England have never done so, though Howard Clark won the individual prize in 1985.

Every time a country staged the World Cup, as it was renamed in 1967, there was an upsurge in the popularity of golf. The World Cup may have done more for the cause of golf worldwide than any other event. 'In a world too often divided by the differences of opinion and conflicting interests, it is heartening to know that representatives of twenty-five countries will be meeting in a spirit of unity and friendly competition to enjoy their favourite sport,' wrote Louis St Laurent, Prime Minister of Canada, in 1955.

Some competitions have been clearly modelled on it. The Men's World Amateur Team Trophy Championship for the Eisenhower Trophy (begun in 1958) is one; another is the Women's World Amateur Team Championship for the Esperito Santo Trophy (begun in 1964).

But as these competitions waxed, the World Cup began to wane. As it entered its third decade it fell foul of the game's increasing commercialism and in 1981 and 1986 it could not be held. The prize-money it offered was small by comparison with other golf events around the world and its prestige, which had been so high at the outset, had dimmed considerably. The International Golf Association took over the running of it and was making brave noises about restoring it to its former glory, starting in 1987. Only time will tell.

The victorious Canadian pair, George Knudson (left) and Al Balding, with the Canada Cup after their win in Rome in 1968.

The Duke of Windsor, a keen golfer, meets Gary Player, Arnold Palmer and Jack Nicklaus at St-Nom-La-Bretèche before the Canada Cup of 1963.

Fijian golfers at the World Cup of 1979.

Bobby Locke playing in a challenge match against Dick Burton at Mere in 1939 and (below) competing in England in 1947 after his highly successful spell in the United States.

I n 1946 Sam Snead won the British Open at St Andrews. The runner-up was Bobby Locke, a South African who later that year beat Snead in a series of 16 challenge matches in South Africa. After he had been walloped 12 – 4, Snead encouraged Locke to try his luck at the pro tour in the US. Thus began the most successful invasion of the US since Harry Vardon 46 years earlier.

Snead knew that Locke would make a lot of money on the US Tour. Locke had twice won the South African Open as an amateur and been the leading amateur in the 1936 Open at Hoylake. He played first in the US Masters and cut quite a dash. He looked ten years older than his age, 29, and his figure was ample, if not yet of Falstaffian proportions. His golf was as distinctive as his plus-fours and the tie he always tucked in beneath the second button of his shirt. He would send his drives and approach shots out to the right before they looped back unerringly to their targets. On the green he putted the eyes out of the ball with a wooden-shafted, rusty headed putter. Locke reckoned that 28 putts each round was enough. Every bit as important as his manner of play was the fact that he was completely imperturbable.

On that first visit to the US he won six events and came second in the money list. He went home to South Africa at the end of the season and returned to the US in 1948 and was just as successful as he had been the previous year. Such plundering of their coffers did not endear him to the Americans and one pro warned him that he had come to the US at a time when the best native-born golfers were in a slump. Locke was later banned from the US Tour on a flimsy technicality.

Thereafter Locke travelled more and more to Europe where he had increasing success. He won the British Open in 1949, thereby starting the Locke era in golf. He won again in 1950 and 1952, and again in 1957 although a curious incident marred this last victory. Locke marked his ball on the 72nd green at St Andrews but replaced it on the wrong spot before holing out for a three-stroke victory over Peter Thomson. The Championship Committee later ruled that as Locke had three for the title from three feet even a two-stroke penalty for replacing his ball would have made no difference. Locke was so relieved that he made a gesture of

Far left *Bobby Locke during the Daks Tournament at Sunningdale in 1955.* Left *Bobby Locke on his way to victory in the 1957 Open at St Andrews and (below left) breaking into song at the presentation ceremony.*

humility. He vowed never again to wear the famous plus-fours that had become as much of a trademark as his measured stride and wooden-shafted putter.

In 1960 Locke was involved in an accident in South Africa when his car was hit by a train at a level crossing. His eyesight was impaired and he never again was a force in international golf. It did not matter. The deeds for which we remember him had long been done. Locke died in March 1987.

His main rival in Europe in the 1950s was Peter Thomson, who was 12 years younger and had begun to emerge while Locke was doing so well in the US. He finished top amateur in the 1948 Australian Open and largely on the strength of this turned pro the next year. Thomson began to look enviously towards Britain. Was he good enough to cut the mustard over there, he wondered? The answer was not long in coming. In 1951 he won the Australian Open, and it was all the encouragement he needed. He came to Britain and finished second, one shot behind Locke, in the Open at Royal Lytham and St Annes.

Two years later he won his first Open, the first by an Australian. By a coincidence the

Amateur was won that year by Douglas Bachli, also an Australian and also a member at Thomson's club, the Victoria in Melbourne. Thomson won again at St Andrews in 1955 when the first prize was £1,000 and the event was televised live by the BBC for the first time. Victory at Hoylake in 1956 stamped his authority on the game. He had become the first player in modern times to win three Championships in a row.

Thomson always wore white shoes, as did Locke. He was a very precise player, as was Locke. But whereas Locke's distinctive characteristic was his banana-shaped shot, Thomson's was his ability to plot his way around any course, particularly links. It is unlikely that he ever hit a shot that he had not thoroughly thought out first.

On well-watered courses he was never at home and for this reason he was not successful on his visits to the US. This led to his not being accepted as a true champion by the Americans. Thomson also did not like the bigger 1.68 in ball. But on hard, fast-running courses where he had to manufacture shots to meet the occasion, he was a master. This was why he did so well in the Open.

At Lytham in 1958 he defeated Dave Thomas, a big-hitting Welshman, in a 36-hole play-off for the Open. He remained a force for many years and in 1965, back at Royal Birkdale, he won his fifth Open. Only Tom Watson has equalled this since the days of the Great Triumvirate. It brought him particular pleasure because the Open had regained its lustre in the eyes of the Americans since Arnold Palmer's arrival in 1960. Thus Thomson's last victory was achieved over a field that contained just about every one of the world's best golfers. A measure of the dominance of the Open by Locke and Thomson is that on average one or other of them won it every other year between 1949 and 1965.

Thomson was highly intelligent and his broad questioning mind made him break out from golf and dabble in politics for a while. Whereas Locke's days were spent in South Africa, Thomson moved into designing and building golf courses in the Far East. He was only lured away from this by the huge prize-money on offer on the US Senior Tour. In 1985 he won more than $350,000 to become the leading money winner. This was more than he had won during all his years as a professional.

Far left *Peter Thomson on the 16th green at Royal Birkdale, just two holes away from his first Open victory in 1954, and (left) he sinks a long putt to complete the first round of his defence of the Open Championship in 1955.*

Peter Thomson at Hoylake during the 1956 Open and (far left) examining his third successive entry in the list of champions.

David Thomas during the play-off for the 1958 Open title.

Victory again for Peter Thomson in 1965, eleven years after his first victory on the same course.

Ben Hogan (left) with
Dutch Harrison (centre)
and Leonard Dodson
(right). All three tied for
first place in the Oakland
Open of 1941.

Byron Nelson takes over
the winning role, receiving
defence bonds as prize
money after the 1941
Miami Open.
Below right Hogan is
back in the money after his
discharge from the armed
forces in 1946 with a win
in the Western Open in St
Louis.

Facing page
Top Ben Hogan on board
the Queen Elizabeth at
Southampton with members
of his Ryder Cup team in
1949. Left to right: Bob
Hamilton, Sam Snead,
Chick Harbert, Jimmy
Demaret, Ben Hogan,
Lloyd Mangrum, Dutch
Harrison, Clayton
Heafner, Johnny Palmer
and Ed Dudley.
Centre The Duchess of
Windsor presents Sam
Snead with the winner's
cheque after his victory in
the 1951 Greenbrier Open.
Bottom Ben Hogan waits
to play his next shot in the
1953 Open at Carnoustie.

lthough the United States Golf Association abandoned amateur events after Pearl Harbor in 1941 and did not reintroduce them until after the end of hostilities, there was more than enough golf in the US during and immediately after the war. At this time two professionals stood head and shoulders above all others. One was small and intense, a former newsboy named Ben Hogan who dominated the pro tour between 1941 and 1943 before joining the Army Air Corps. This left the way clear for Byron Nelson, another Texan. Nelson entered 51 events in the 24 months in question. He won eight in 1944 and 18 in 1945. Eleven of his successes in 1945 came in a row, including the US PGA.

After the war Hogan returned to carry on where he had left off. For all the efforts of Nelson, who was to go into semi-retirement that year, of Sam Snead, British Open Champion in 1946, of Bobby Locke of South Africa, and of half a dozen other pros, Hogan was unapproachable from now on. He took his first US PGA in 1946 when he was 33, his first US Open two years later. Thus started the Age of Hogan.

It almost ended within a few months. What happened on that fateful February morning in 1949 has been made into a film and formed the basis of dozens of newspaper and magazine articles. He and his wife Valerie crashed in head-on collision with a bus. Hogan suffered a double fracture of his pelvis, a fractured collarbone, a broken bone in his left ankle and a broken right rib. A month later complications set in. Blood clots developed in his legs.

He was a very sick man, liable to bouts of delirium during which he would go through the motions of gripping and regripping a golf club and tossing blades of grass in the air to test the wind direction. In his delirium he would blurt out 'Back on the left, back on the left', as though he was talking to wayward spectators. When he was discharged from hospital after 58 days on his back, he weighed little more than a child, a mere 6½ stone (41 kg).

Even with his legendary determination it was a surprise that he recovered sufficiently to be non-playing captain of the US Ryder Cup team that narrowly beat Britain and Ireland at Ganton, Yorkshire, that summer. But that was as nothing to the astonishment that reverberated

around the golf world when Hogan tied with Snead for first place in the first event of 1950, the Los Angeles Open, less than a year after his fearful accident.

In June, Hogan entered the US Open. His injuries had left him prone to cramp and each morning he would wrap his legs with elastic bandages and limp slowly down the fairways of the Merion club outside Philadelphia. Even so, he came to the 72nd needing a par four to tie with Lloyd Mangrum and George Fazio. Hogan managed it and then cruised to victory in the next day's play-off.

He was now as complete a golfer as any who had ever lived: long off the tee, sound on the greens and able to reproduce any stroke as he required it. It was entirely fitting that when the Open was staged at Oakland Hills, Detroit, the most difficult course the pros had played until then, it was Hogan, the reigning Masters Champion, who triumphed. 'I'm glad I brought this monster to its knees', he growled at the victory ceremony after rounds of 76, 73, 71 and 67.

Hogan's greatest year came in 1953 when he went close to matching Bobby Jones's feat in 1930 of winning four major championships. In Jones's day they had been the Amateur and Open Championships of Britain and the US, the Impregnable Quadrilateral as they became known. By Hogan's time the two Amateur Championships had been replaced by the US Masters and the US PGA.

Hogan played flawlessly to win the US Masters at Augusta and then the US Open at Oakmont, the fabled course near Pittsburgh. In July he crossed the Atlantic to Scotland to compete in the Open at Carnoustie, the first Open he had ever entered. He was typically thorough. He would practise each day and then walk the course backwards – from green to tee – each night after dinner.

He came safely through the pre-qualifying and after two rounds lay on 144, two strokes behind the leaders. At the time two rounds were played on the last day, which was cold, windy and grey. Hogan had a penicillin injection against a touch of 'flu and then went out and scored 70 in the morning and 68, a course record, after lunch. He won his third major championship of the year by four shots.

He seemed able to summon up his best play just when he wanted it most. After Hogan's victory at Carnoustie Bernard Darwin noted: 'If

The Hogan swing.

he had needed a 64 you were quite certain he would have played a 64. Hogan gave you the distinct impression he was capable of getting whatever score was needed to win.'

    Although he was not to win another major championship, Hogan competed for a few more years: his trademarks, a white cap and narrowed eyes, not to mention his wonderfully accurate golf, still drew the crowds. In 1960 he made a tremendous bid for the US Open and it was only a bravura performance by a powerful and fearless young man that denied Hogan a

Ben Hogan receives a civic reception from the mayor of New York after returning from Britain where he had added the British Open title to the US Open which he had won earlier in the year.

Byron Nelson (extreme left) with the next generation of big money-winners on the US circuit. Left to right: Byron Nelson, Tommy Jacobs, Billy Casper, Don January, Johnny Pott, Tony Lema, Ken Venturi, Dave Marr, Gene Littler, Julius Boros, Arnold Palmer.

fifth Open. That man's name was Arnold Palmer. Jack Nicklaus, then still an amateur, finished runner-up.

Clearly the writing was on the wall for the great Texan. In nearly twenty years at the top he had won the US Open four times, the US Masters and US PGA Championships twice and the British Open once. 'Nobody covered the flag like he did', said Gene Sarazen by way of tribute. But a new age was beginning: it was the Age of Arnold Palmer and Jack Nicklaus.

The US Ryder Cup team arrive at London Airport in 1957.
Left to right: Jackie Burke, Tommy Bolt, Doug Ford, Ed Furgol, Dow Finsterwald, Lionel Hebert, Fred Hawkins, Dick Mayer, Ted Kroll and Art Wall.

t is interesting how things go in cycles. The normal cycle of one American victory after another in the Ryder Cup has been broken twice since the war, each time after intervals of a quarter of a century. The first occasion was in October 1957, 24 years after the last victory. Dai Rees, the spiky little Welshman, was captain and it was held at Lindrick in Yorkshire.

The second occasion – as if anyone did not know this – was 28 years later, at The Belfry in September 1985. There the similarities end, for whereas the recent victory became a probability the moment the 1983 team went so close (they were ahead or level until late in the afternoon of the last day and ultimately only lost by one point), victory for Dai Rees's men came like a bolt from the blue. 'It was the third British victory since the series began in 1926 and the biggest', wrote Our Golf Correspondent in *The Times*. 'Frankly, you could have knocked us all down with a feather.'

Compared with the variety of play nowadays, the competition was blessedly simple in 1957. One day of foursomes and a second day of singles. That was it. No wretched fourballs and all matches played over 36 holes, the proper distance, one that practically guarantees an accurate result. No television, very little radio and yards and yards of column inches in the papers.

The Americans love to pretend they have not the faintest idea how to play foursomes. They call them 'Scotch foursomes' and talk of players 'alternately hitting every shot with one ball', which says as much for their grasp of the English language as it does for their knowledge of this form of golf. Perhaps they really do not know what they are doing and, if so, is this a strength? They always win the foursomes, it seems.

It has been so wherever there have been Ryder, Walker and Curtis Cups and so it was at Lindrick. The Americans won the foursomes three matches to one: Doug Ford and Dow Finsterwald by 2 and 1 over Peter Alliss and Bernard Hunt; Dick Mayer and Tommy Bolt (he of the terrible temperament) by 7 and 5 over Christy O'Connor and Eric Brown; and Ted Kroll and Jackie Burke, the American captain, by 4 and 3 over Harry Weetman and Max Faulkner. The only home winners were Dai Rees and Ken Bousfield, who defeated Art Wall

Dai Rees, the British captain, greets his American counterpart Jackie Burke.

The British Ryder Cup team of 1957.
Back, left to right: Harry Bradshaw, Peter Mills, Peter Alliss, Bernard Hunt, Harry Weetman.
Front: Max Faulkner, Eric Brown, Dai Rees, Ken Bousfield, Christy O'Connor.

Dick Mayer (left) on his way to an impressive win with his partner Tommy Bolt over Eric Brown (right) and Christy O'Connor on the first day.

95

Dai Rees congratulates his partner Ken Bousfield after they had recorded the only British win in the foursomes.

Lionel Hebert concedes victory to Ken Bousfield in their singles match.

Dai Rees, the victorious captain.

and Fred Hawkins 3 and 2.

So, at the halfway point of the 12th Ryder Cup, history seemed to be repeating itself. The Americans led by three matches to one and you would have got very long odds indeed against Britain winning the next day. But what do they say about golf? 'The only predictable thing about golf is its unpredictability.' A wind got up that Friday night making Lindrick a different golf course for the singles on the second day, one that was two or three shots harder than it had been the previous day. The next morning the Americans, who had been so strong on Friday, were sent reeling.

By the time the eight matches reached the 5th green the British were up in seven and all square in the eighth. They had won 16 holes to their opponents' seven. The British team completed the first 50 holes played in eight under fours while the Americans were 11 over fours.

Nowhere was Britain's revival better portrayed than by Rees himself. The captain had taken a risk in playing himself ahead of Harry Weetman but he overran Ed Furgol and won 7 and 6. That was the same margin of victory as Christy O'Connor's over Finsterwald, clinched by a superlative burst during which he took eight of the first 11 holes after lunch.

Surely the American team would fight back? Their strength was in their tail, a typical American practice to make sure that the competition was not lost by the less-experienced players. But no. Burke, Bolt, Furgol and Hebert, sounding like a firm of West End solicitors, were all off form and well beaten. 'To whichever ringside one stumbled, the spectacle was the same on that frenzied afternoon', noted *The Times*. 'Britain were holing the putts, the Americans were missing them. The argument that America's best players were left behind does not ring true. No place can be gained in their team without constant proof of great ability. It is true that the team did not contain famous names but reputation is no guarantee of success. Snead and Mangrum had reputations at Wentworth in 1953 and lost their singles; Middlecoff had one two years ago and lost. Burke, this year, stood highest in his opponents' esteem and was beaten by 7 and 6.'

Ford finished like a tired man in the morning, dropping shots on the last three holes before lunch to allow Hunt back in. That was

Christy O'Connor and (far left) Max Faulkner in action at Lindrick.

the last the American saw of Hunt who went on to win 6 and 5. There was a measure of iron in the Englishman's victory. It went some way towards redeeming the loss to the Americans in the 1953 Ryder Cup, a loss attributed to the disappointing play of Hunt and Alliss, both of whom were making their débuts.

And so Britain won by 7½ points to 4½. A footnote to their victory was added by Tommy Bolt who accused the British crowd of unsporting behaviour because 'they cheered every time I missed a putt'. That struck a chord with those who were at The Belfry in 1985. The man who made a suitably elegant response on behalf of the British public at Lindrick was none other than Lord Brabazon of Tara. 'I have great sympathy with him but what is a crowd to do when their hero wins a hole by virtue of the "enemy" missing a putt?' he wrote in a letter to *The Times*. He went on:

'Let us take the case of the Cup's fate being dependent on one last match. Both balls lie about six feet from the hole. The Englishman misses his, the American misses. Is the crowd to remain mute for fear of cheering a missed putt, and being dubbed unsporting? Surely it is straining human nature too much?'

Such manners, wrote Vernon Crudge from New York City, were nothing new. 'Walter Hagen, just failing to hole a short chip to tie the British Open in 1923, says in his entertaining book (*The Walter Hagen Story*)....'The huge gallery of Britishers applauded loudly because England surely needed a win in their Open.'

They surely did, just as they needed and deserved victory in the Ryder Cup in 1957 – and again in 1985. As for the latter, well that's another story.

Henry Cotton competing with Norman von Nida during the News of the World Match-Play in 1947.

Antonio Garrido (left) and Billy Casper wait on the tee during the Benson & Hedges International at Fulford in 1977.

If you can tell a man by the books he keeps on his shelves, what can you tell from the quality of the golf tournaments on which the European Tour was built? At the very least they represent a fleeting entry in the business ledger, a symbol of healthy financial days. At best, their names are written into the fabric of British golf.

In 1903 the average working wage was £1 a week. Few professional golfers had higher weekly retainers than ten shillings (50p) and many had none at all. Tuition cost no more than five shillings (25p) an hour, the average club subscription was £3 a year and a brand-new wood cost 12s 6d (62p).

Imagine, then, the interest generated by the announcement that Mr (later Sir) Emsley Carr, proprietor of the *News of the World*, had offered £200 for a match-play golf tournament among professionals. Imagine what Vardon, Ray and Braid must have said. The prize-money, no matter how paltry it seems now, represented a considerable amount in those days. It was ten times as much as for any previous tournament.

Generous as the offer was, it was not made from blind philanthropy. Carr was a keen golfer and so was his associate, George Riddell, who owned Walton Heath Golf Club. The *NoW*, a newspaper with strong sporting instincts, had just begun a golf instructional series by J.H. Taylor and was celebrating its Diamond Jubilee. How better to mark the occasion than by launching a golf tournament?

Quite why it was decided to make it match-play instead of stroke-play is not clear. Probably the same values applied then as now, namely that the red meat of man-to-man combat is more exciting than the white meat of four rounds of stroke-play. Regional qualifying rounds were arranged to provide 32 places for match-play at Walton Heath in October and in the final James Braid beat Ted Ray, winning £100 for doing so. In following years the prize-money was increased to provide as much as £5 for second-round losers.

The tournament, the first to be commercially sponsored, was a roaring success, generating innumerable mentions of the *NoW* among spectators and players and helping also to create considerable interest in the Professional Golfers' Association. Within a few years the PGA had grown sufficiently for it to create

A young spectator retrieves Dai Rees's ball from the cup after he had holed for an eagle two during the News of the World Match-Play Championship at Hoylake in 1946.

Welsh, West of England and East Anglian sections. Indirectly, too, the *NoW* PGA Championship led to the formation of a co-operative trading society.

For more than sixty years the *NoW* continued to sponsor the event, which in 1946 became known as the British PGA Match-Play Championship. Its roll of winners includes the most famous golfers of succeeding generations. The names ring out like bells: Braid, Taylor, Vardon, Cotton, Percy Alliss (father of Peter), Rees, Faulkner, Thomson. Almost the only significant player not to have won this prestigious and enduring tournament was Ted Ray, who was runner-up three times.

In 1969 the *NoW* ceased their sponsorship and the tournament passed through a succession of hands including Long John Whisky, manufacturers of Scotch; Benson & Hedges, at the same time as they also sponsored their own stroke-play tournament, and Sun Alliance, also sponsors of the Ryder Cup in 1979 and 1981.

Somewhat shorter was the history of the Penfold Tournament, the first of which Percy Alliss won at Royal Porthcawl in 1932. For a baker's dozen years from the mid-Fifties

the event was known as the Swallow-Penfold when Swallow Ltd shared the sponsorship. It reverted to its original name from 1967 until its demise in 1974.

There are some tournaments whose long-term survival was doubtful almost from the start. The Alcan International Championship lasted a mere four years during which three championships were played. The Bob Hope British Classic was held for only four years, as was the Coral Classic.

On the other hand, another distinguished event, both in content and longevity, was the Daks. The name belongs to Simpsons, the well-known London men's shop. Dr Leonard Simpson believed that well-dressed pro golfers would help to sell his product and hence began the Daks Tournament. It lasted from 1950 until 1971. This was undoubtedly a successful theory though it is one of life's pleasing ironies that Neil Coles, who won the Daks a record four times, is a man to whom sartorial elegance does not come quite so easily as it does to, say, Doug Sanders or Max Faulkner. Coles would seldom venture out at Wentworth, where the Daks was always played, or anywhere else come to think of it, in anything

Bill Large watches Peter
Alliss putt during the
Martini International at
Long Ashton in 1966.

Piccadilly were lavish in the
facilities which they
provided for the contestants
in their World Match-Play
tournament.

less than dark sweaters, dark trousers and dark if
not black shoes.

In 1946, Dunlop started the Dunlop
Masters Tournament, an élite event modelled on
the small affair that takes place in Georgia each
spring: a small field, international players, past
winners. For all but forty years it was run with
precision and grace, an exception among the
run-of-the-mill 72-hole stroke-play events. All
good things must come to an end, however.
Dunlop's finances took a battering in the early
Eighties and this tournament, charming and

Watney Mann sponsor their own golfing challenge.

Senior Service provide hospitality for the competitors by the 1st tee in their tournament.
Left to right: Dai Rees, Bill Large, Peter Thomson and Dave Ragan.

engaging as it was, was a casualty. It was taken over by Dunhill, the cigarette manufacturers, and renamed the Dunhill British Masters.

With a tented village, American players being imported at considerable expense, and Concorde laid on to sweep competitors to the US Open the moment the event was concluded, the Dunhill British Masters was light years away from Emsley Carr's News of the World Tournament. But then golf had come a long way, too.

unicipal is not a word that is pleasing to the ear. It smacks of munitions, which makes it rather warlike, or munificence, which suggests something that it is not. Abbreviated to 'muni' it can be said with a curled lip and a sneer: 'So you play at a muni, eh? Well, more fool you.'

Thousands of golfers in Britain play on courses that are open to anyone, courses where you just turn up, book your tee time and off you go. There are more than 200 in Britain and the body to which many belong, the National Golf Courses Association, was founded in 1927. One of its founding members was J.H. Taylor, four times winner of the Open and one of the Great Triumvirate.

The most famous public course in the world is St Andrews where four-balls go off every ten minutes almost every daylight hour. Woe betide you if you have not booked a tee time in advance. Carnoustie is municipally owned, too, though there is marginally less pressure there than on the Old Course at the 'Home of Golf'.

Municipal in this context means belonging to the local governing authority of a city or town. In the post-war period, as Britain struggled back to health and prosperity, municipal golf courses did not suddenly sprout all over the country. The theory behind them was that to provide golf on the rates was no more unusual than to provide swimming baths or libraries and where the experiment did go ahead, several hundred golfers made their first faltering attempts at playing the game on such public courses as Brand Hall (1946) in Worcestershire and Bromley (1948) in Kent.

The problem was that in difficult times like these theories did not always count for much. There may have been land for development but where was the money to develop the land? Golf was slow to benefit from people's increased leisure time and from the advances in equipment. It remained a sport that had built its popularity on a narrow base. Two things changed this state of affairs. Arnold Palmer entered the Open in 1960 and won it in 1961 and 1962, thereby re-establishing the importance of the game's oldest major championship; and BBC Television began to cover golf in a big way. That is how the popularity of the game became more widespread.

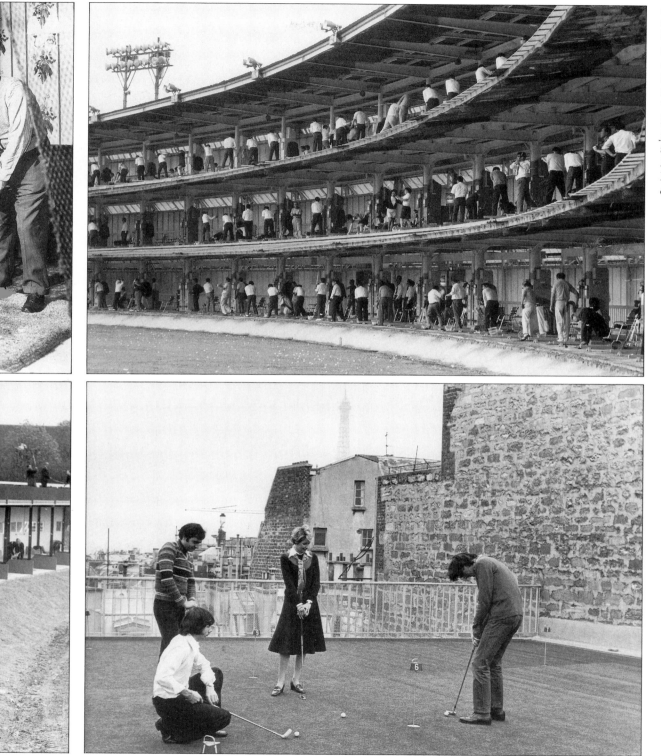

Practice facilities for an ever-growing golf fraternity.
Far left *Golf clinic in the cocktail bar at the Starcross Hotel in Barnsley.*
Left *The massive driving range at Shiba Park, Tokyo.*
Below far left *Britain's first automatic day and night golf centre in Finchley.*
Below left *Putting practice on a roof in Paris.*

Target golf at Hanover, Massachusetts.

Golf dome on Wormwood Scrubs Common and (far right) the relevant price list.

Here are some examples of what then happened to the growth of golf courses. The first is of a large new club in the south of England. It had one championship course and another was being designed. It had been planned in the property boom of the early 1970s and its owners spent £1.5 million on 400 acres (162 ha) of prime heather and birch golfing country. But times changed too soon and too quickly.

It failed to attract enough visitors and the profits which needed to be as high as 25 per cent to cope with the high interest and repayment rates, were half that amount. The club was put up for sale within a few years of opening. 'We built an expensive course, spent a lot of money on it and we didn't get the return we wanted,' said one of the bosses. 'Anyone who builds a big course and a big clubhouse today is in trouble.' It looked as out of date as an art deco high street cinema.

More common and making more financial sense were the new purpose-built courses such as Redbourn near St Albans where costs are pared to the bone, and golf centres that can provide a floodlit driving range, an 18-hole course, a pitch-and-putt facility, a putting green and bar and food facilities. All this could be fitted into a site of 150 acres (61 ha).

Also increasing in popularity are joint ventures between local authorities and expert companies in the leisure business. For example, Redditch Corporation gave a developer 220 acres (89 ha) on which to build a golf course, equestrian centre and fishing lake. The money the firm received from selling land on which 150 houses could be built helped to generate money to finance the project. It was a technique that was used at Livingston in Scotland and at Ingle in Lancashire.

Some of the more modest municipal courses can make money, even though precious few of them do. Thorpe Wood, near Peterborough, is a 6,600 yd (6,035 m) course built by Peterborough Development Corporation at a cost of £250,000. The PDC run the course as a thoroughly commercial enterprise, not seeing it in any way as a cheap amenity for ratepayers. They employ two professionals and give them almost total control. Season tickets, so common at municipal courses, are banned. At the weekend, singles are not allowed. Scorecards carry advertising. Practice is charged for. The end result of this is that Thorpe Wood was making such a success of itself that a

GOLF DOME

Driving Range	25 Balls	20p
	100 Balls	70p
Putting Course	18 Holes	20p
Vistagolf		each per Hour
	2 Persons	60p
	4 Persons	40p
Club Hire	1 Wood	10p
	1 Iron	
Lessons	per ½ Hr.	100p

second course was added scarcely more than five years after the first was opened.

Traditionally, Britain's municipal courses have been looked down upon by the private clubs. It is now the case that clubs like Thorpe Wood, Meyrick Park in Bournemouth, Beckenham Place Park and Addington Court, where Geoff Cotton has 52 full-time employees under his direction as well as two 18-hole courses both in sparkling condition all the year round, are showing more than a few private clubs how to survive.

Philomena Garvey, an important win on the first day in 1952.

You would have got very long odds indeed against a British victory in the Curtis Cup at Muirfield in 1952. In boxing parlance it looked as though it would be a one-round affair, the US having won or tied all the five previous encounters. British golf was generally at a low ebb: not since the Walker Cup of 1938, held at St Andrews, had there been a British success in the Walker, Curtis or Ryder Cups.

But what was this? The Ladies' Golf Union was announcing a squad of probables more than half a year before the match. No team from Britain had been picked so early before. In November 1951 Lady Kathleen Cairns, a professional tennis and squash coach, was named non-playing captain and 10 others were chosen from whom the team would be selected. At this time the Curtis Cup competition consisted of one day of foursomes and one day of singles, played between sides of six chosen from eight players.

Another indication that the selectors were being unusually thorough came soon after Christmas when it was announced that the chosen 10 players had been invited to Muirfield. Trials would be held during the week and the team would be named at the end of it.

The Americans had selected a young and inexperienced team with an average age of 25. Only Dorothy Kirby, the US Amateur Champion, and Polly Riley had played in the Curtis Cup before and they had both played twice.

The two teams reached Muirfield early in June. It was cold and windy on that part of the Scottish coast and neither side found matters entirely to their liking. The Americans had difficulty in coping with the stiff wind that blew off the Firth of Forth; the British found that the effect of practising behind closed doors was eerie. They had anticipated noisy, patriotic spectators.

In the opening day's 36-hole foursomes, Britain felt confident enough to do without Kitty McCann, the British Amateur Champion, and Jeanne Bisgood, the English Amateur Champion, relying on the old hands who had been heavily defeated at Buffalo two years earlier. Only one newcomer, Moira Paterson, was selected for the foursomes.

Enthusiastic cheering was to be heard from all points of the course as the day wore on.

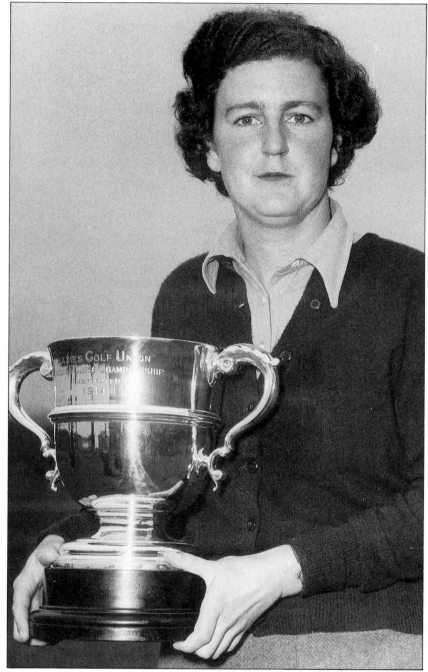

Jean Donald and Elizabeth Price won 3 and 2, Donald ending it with a 30-foot putt that plunged into the heart of the hole. The Americans levelled in the second match but were always up against it in the third foursomes. Polly Riley and Patricia O'Sullivan, though longer off the tee, were trailing Philomena Garvey and Moira Paterson until the 30th hole when they took the lead for the first time. By the 34th, Britain had regained the lead and they won 2 and 1. It was an important point to win, for the Americans were an experienced pair. If it did nothing else it indicated that even the toughest of the Americans were beatable.

From Saturday's six singles Britain needed three wins to be sure of overall victory. By lunch they were ahead in four, level in one and down in the last. In the afternoon Donald let slip the two-hole lead she had held at lunch, streaked into a commanding lead only to lose it all and finish one down. It was a disappointing result for Britain and for Donald whose home course of North Berwick was only a drive and a mid-iron away. Some of the damage was repaired by Frances (Bunty) Stephens who won a 2 and 1 victory.

The second point of the day was won

Above Jeanne Bisgood *and (above left) Kitty McCann, key members of the 1952 Curtis Cup team.*

*Elizabeth Price, a vital role
in the 1952 victory and
Ladies' Champion in 1959.*

Elizabeth Price, a vital role in the 1952 victory and Ladies' Champion in 1959.

by Jeanne Bisgood who gave quite a hiding to May Murray. But as Philomena Garvey, one of the heroines of the first day, lost to Clare Doran the match depended on the last pair, Elizabeth Price and the small and young Grace de Moss. The American was only 17 and the responsibility of playing last must have weighed on her shoulders.

It was a severe test for Elizabeth Price, too, for she was fighting to stave off stomach sickness. Price, who had for many years received daily treatment for diabetes, was told on the 27th hole that the result depended on her. She was all-square at the time. Four holes later she took the lead. Then de Moss contracted the golfer's nightmare, the socket. At the 32nd hole she socketed and was so startled that she lost that hole and the next two and with it the match.

Angela Bonallack, a leading lady in British golf in the 1960s though never to enjoy a Curtis Cup victory.

'Gentlemen: the toast is the ladies' health and prosperity,' was how one newspaper correspondent began his report of Britain's first victory in the Curtis Cup. 'This will cause some stir back home,' said the American captain, who probably was not relishing her new status as the first losing American captain. 'Some of our administrators won't be able to understand it.'

It was not a fluke. Moira Paterson's victory a few weeks later in the British Amateur at Troon confirmed this. The Curtis Cup victory was a well-executed performance by a well-prepared team and the idea of selecting players far in advance and letting them spend a week together should have been handed down from one team to the next. Unfortunately it was not. Perhaps that is why it took more than thirty years before Britain won the Curtis Cup again.

*Marley Spearman celebrates
as her final putt ensures that
the British team retain the
Commonwealth Women's
Golf Trophy at Melbourne
in 1963.*

PART FOUR

YEARS OF FAME AND FORTUNE,
1960–1974

rnold Palmer's influence on golf reached all corners of the globe. Unlike Ben Hogan, who was as coldly calculating as he was dominant in the 1950s, Palmer had a warmth about him that was instantly appealing to an American public yearning for a hero. The golf glove stuffed casually in his hip pocket when he putted and the carelessly tossed cigarette set a fashion at all levels of the game and it was said, with some truth, that more people would watch Palmer change his shoes in the car park than would follow some lesser mortal while he completed a round of 66.

It was in 1960 that Palmer's full competitive powers first caught the imagination. He had already won the Masters once, in 1958, but on this second occasion at Augusta National, he came to the last three holes needing two birdies to win from Ken Venturi – and got them.

Thus was born the legendary 'Arnold Palmer charge' and soon there was to be 'Arnie's Army' as well when, just two months later, he took his one and only United States Open Championship at Cherry Hills in Denver. This was equally spectacular since with only one round to play he stood seven strokes behind Mike Souchak.

In those days 36 holes were still played on the last day and over a brief lunch Palmer asked a reporter friend of his, Bob Drum, whether he still had a chance. 'None whatsoever,' Drum replied emphatically. Perhaps that was just the spur Palmer needed. He promptly went out and drove the 1st green, which was a par four, got his three, picked up five more birdies to the turn and was out in 30. He finished in 65 and won by two strokes from Jack Nicklaus, who at the time was still an amateur.

For some years the British Open had rather lost its world standing but 1960 was, by happy chance, its centenary year and Palmer, committed already to representing the United States in the old Canada Cup at Portmarnock just before – and helping Sam Snead to win it – could not resist the temptation of going for his third major championship of that year.

Only Ben Hogan, in 1953, had ever won the Masters, US Open and British Open in the same season, and although Palmer failed to match the achievement, losing by a stroke to Kel Nagle of Australia at St Andrews, his appetite

Arnold Palmer, one shot ahead of Kel Nagle and on his way to his first Open victory at Royal Birkdale in 1961.

BY ROWLAND HILDER

Come to Britain
for GOLF

Published by the Travel Association of Great Britain and Northern Ireland (Tourist Division of the British Tourist and Holidays Board) and printed in Great Britain by W. S. Cowell Ltd, London & Ipswich.

A Rowland Hilder poster for the Travel Association of Great Britain and Northern Ireland.

Spectacular golf courses around the world.
Right *Genuine desert rock and scrub surround the well-watered patches of green on the La Quinta course at Palm Springs.*
Below *The rugged challenge of Rye on the Kent coast.*
Below right *Deceptive light gives the normally lush green of Lahinch, on Ireland's west coast, an arid desert appearance.*

The undulating beauty of Shinnecock Hills, one of America's longest established courses.

Above *The exquisitely manicured course at Augusta National.* Left *Early morning at La Manga in southern Spain.*

Right *In the days before video Archie Compston offered his advice at 78 rpm.*
Far right *Souvenirs of great occasions. Post-war austerity is reflected in the programme for the 1949 Open at Royal St George's.*

Henry Cotton and Jack Nicklaus — golfers of world stature and worthy of front-cover treatment on any magazine.

A golfing Donald Duck stands among the comics which frequently portrayed the perils of life on the golf course.

had been whetted. He wanted this, the oldest of all the game's titles, and because he wanted it, so others wanted it too.

A year later Palmer was back and, in appalling weather at Royal Birkdale, he revealed not only strength of hand and body but strength of purpose as well with a one-stroke victory from Dai Rees. Then, at Troon in 1962 and this time in hot, sunny weather and on a fast-running course, he destroyed the field finishing six strokes clear of Nagle and no less than 13 in front of Brian Huggett and Phil Rodgers.

More significantly the Open Championship had been re-born, regaining the status it had enjoyed in the days of Walter Hagen, Bobby Jones and Gene Sarazen in the 1920s and early '30s. Americans came over in ever-increasing numbers and the Royal and Ancient matched their arrival with ever-increasing prize-money. They also appointed Keith Mackenzie as secretary in 1967 and they found in him the ideal 'front man'. When Palmer played in his first Open the total prize-money was £7,000.. When Mackenzie took over it was £15,000. Three years later, in 1970, it had reached £40,000 and by 1980 it was £200,000. Nor is there much sign of the pace slacking for

in 1987 it was £650,000, though by then Mackenzie had retired and been succeeded by Michael Bonallack, a considerable amateur golfer in his time.

The growth of the American Tour could also be traced to the years of Arnold Palmer. In 1958, when he was leading money-winner, his earnings for the season were $75,000. In 1986, when Greg Norman of Australia became the first overseas winner since Gary Player in 1961, he received $653,000 while his worldwide earnings exceeded $1 million.

Even these sums are only a part of the huge financial iceberg, for Palmer's other indirect contribution to the game was that he caught the imagination of a Cleveland lawyer, Mark McCormack. Players had had managers before, notably Sam Snead, whose affairs were managed by Fred Corcoran, but McCormack made golf into really big business.

Gary Player and Jack Nicklaus, for a time, were also among McCormack's early clients, and today his International Management Group looks after a vast stable of not only golfers but other sportsmen, film stars and television entertainers. What McCormack was able to do for Palmer was to turn his earnings on

Victory again for Arnold Palmer at Troon in 1962.

Arnold Palmer plays the charming host to invited members of 'Arnie's Army'.

Arnold Palmer strides towards the World Match-Play title in 1967.

Still winning in 1975. Arnold Palmer enjoys watching his final putt sink to win the PGA Championship at Royal St George's at the age of 45.

the golf course into a financial empire of its own.

Palmer was the first man to win more than $1 million, the target being passed in 1968 when he tied second in the US PGA Championship, an event incidentally that has always eluded him. But it had taken him 13 years to reach the $1 million figure, whereas today it takes much lesser golfers only a fraction of that time. What McCormack, and now other managers, are increasingly able to do is to multiply their client's earnings on the course many times over from other sources.

Palmer, though he continues to live in his native Latrobe in Pennsylvania, quickly became a pilot and in his time has flown everything from a 747 to a simulated lunar module. With his own aircraft he was able to cut down his travelling time, landing only a mile or two from his home which he would call up on the radio to say that he was about to land and a car would then go to meet him.

There are nevertheless pressures to such a way of life and Palmer's reign at the top of the golfing tree was relatively brief. In 1962 he tied for the US Open but lost the play-off to Nicklaus, who had only just turned professional. It seemed unthinkable at the time for only a month or two earlier Palmer had won the US Masters for a third time and in 1964 he won it for a then-record fourth time. His star was nevertheless on the wane and his most bitter disappointment was in the US Open of 1966 at Olympic, San Francisco, when he lost a seven-stroke lead with nine holes to play against Billy Casper and was then beaten in the play-off.

There were tournament wins, of course – 61 in all – and wherever he went Palmer would always draw a large and enthusiastic crowd. There is still, even now, a special sound to an Arnold Palmer birdie and a special expectancy as he strides on to the tee, hitches up his trousers and flexes those formidable forearms.

No-one has been more responsible for giving golf the mass appeal it has today.

Roberto de Vicenzo and Kel Nagle (below), two men to whom a small inaccuracy on the scorecard became a major disaster.

Golf can be as cruel as it can also be rewarding but it can seldom have been as cruel as it was to that most gentle and charming of Argentinians, Roberto de Vicenzo, in the 1968 Masters at Augusta. The year before he had won the Open Championship at Hoylake and now, on his 45th birthday, he had tied and faced a play-off with Bob Goalby for one of the great prizes of American golf. Or so it seemed; but appearances are deceptive.

The dust had not even settled on his brilliant last round of 65, the news of it already being flashed to the far-flung corners of the globe, when it became evident that something seriously was amiss. Green-jacketed officials of Augusta National could be seen hurrying to the cabin where, in those days, an ailing Bobby Jones always spent the week of the Masters. Newspaper reporters, already dictating their graphic accounts, were advised to 'hold it'.

At length and with great sadness the news had to be broken that de Vicenzo, in the heat of understandable excitement, had failed to notice that his partner had marked him down for a four at the 17th instead of the birdie three he had scored. His 65, to which all the golfing world was witness, either there or on television, consequently became the 66 for which he had signed, and instead of tieing he had lost, by a stroke.

The rules of golf were scoured from end to end to find some possible loophole. They were quite unforgiving. A player who signs for a score higher than the number of strokes he has taken must stand by it while if he signs for one lower, he shall be disqualified. The total does not matter, only his scores at each hole.

De Vicenzo had only himself to blame. He simply did not notice, his vision do doubt blurred by tears of joy, the adrenalin still pumping. 'What a stupid I am,' was his disarming summing-up of an otherwise joyous last round that had begun with his holing his second shot to the 1st green for an eagle two which prompted the gallery to sing 'Happy Birthday'. It was hardly that at the day's end but the 1968 Masters will always be remembered as de Vicenzo's rather than Goalby's.

Such errors with the card and pencil are not uncommon. An almost equally notorious incident occurred in the 1969 Alcan Golfer of the Year tournament at Portland, Oregon. Kel Nagle of Australia had been lying in second

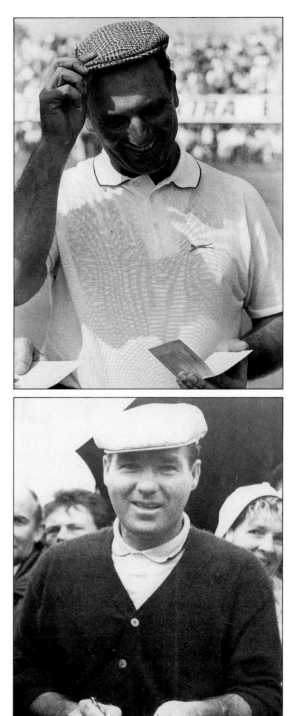

place after the first round and was still well to the fore after 36 holes.

As with de Vicenzo, however, he failed to scrutinize his card carefully enough. His partner, glancing no doubt at a whole string of threes and fours, marked Nagle as having taken 35 to the turn. But he had put the figures in the wrong square, against the 9th hole. Again the officials had no option but to accept that the Australian had somehow expended 35 strokes at that one hole and had therefore taken 105 for the round.

If these are just two examples of how cruel golf can be, it is also a game which can occasionally relent just when this seems impossible. Ken Venturi's victory in the 1964 US Open, at Congressional, provided just such a moment. A gifted amateur who in 1956 had led the Masters through its first three rounds, he had had instant success when subsequently he turned professional.

Only a sensational finish by Arnold Palmer had robbed him of another Masters in 1960 and already he was being hailed as 'another Byron Nelson', the 'next Ben Hogan' and 'better than Sam Snead'. Such adulation needs handling and perhaps Venturi could not handle it. He stopped winning and in three years he found himself almost begging to play in tournaments run by sponsors who previously could not wait to get his entry form.

In the midst of this slump he had also suffered innocent injury. While picking his ball out of a hole during the Palm Springs Classic, he experienced an excruciating pain in his chest. Doctors were unable to diagnose the problem but for weeks Venturi could not raise his right arm high enough to comb his hair. He did his best to keep playing but his swing became a shambles and remained a shambles even when the pain left him.

By degrees he nevertheless began slowly to pick up the pieces again and it is possible that the depths to which he had sunk were also the making of him. No-one had considered him as a possible winner of the US Open amid the steamy heat of a Washington summer and still less so when he trailed Tommy Jacobs by six strokes and Arnold Palmer by five after 36 holes.

The last two rounds were then still being played on a single day and that Saturday morning Venturi was a man inspired: out in 30, round in 66 with two bogeys at the last two

holes and now within two shots of Jacobs. There was nevertheless a reason for those two bogeys. Venturi had neglected to take any salt tablets and, in the intense heat, he became so dehydrated that he was unable to eat any lunch.

A doctor was called who ordered him

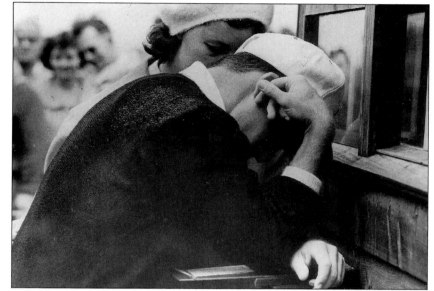

to lie down in the shade of the locker room while he administered salt and iced tea to replenish the lost liquids in his system. There were serious doubts about his ability to play another 18 holes in the afternoon and as a precaution a doctor accompanied him carrying a thermos of iced tea and towels soaked in water which he kept placing round Venturi's neck.

'That last round became my whole life,' reflected Venturi later. 'I never really knew where I was. I was like a robot. I just kept going, going, going. I would just keep moving from the tee to the ball to the green and somehow the ball just kept going straight.'

He refused to look at the scoreboards but, as he came to the 18th tee, he did at last ask a friend how he was placed. 'All you gotta do is stand on your feet,' he was told. 'You're four strokes ahead.' Even so he was utterly exhausted, his eyes downcast and his feet as heavy as lead. At that moment, every muscle in his body was crying out for relief as he trudged the final fairway. Joe Dey, an official of the US Tour, urged him: 'Hold your head up, Ken, you're a champion now.' Slowly Venturi raised his eyes, removed his white cap, heard at last the crowd's applause and inwardly wept.

Ken Venturi, a great battler against the odds.
Top *Gary Player is comforted by his wife after he had dropped two shots at the final hole at Muirfield in 1959 and thought his chance had gone. As it was his score was still good enough to give him his first Open title.*

When Jack Nicklaus won the Masters at Augusta for the second time in 1965 with rounds of 67, 71, 64 and 69 for a record aggregate of 271, he was paid the ultimate tribute by Bobby Jones, certainly the greatest amateur who has ever lived and, in the opinion of some, the finest golfer of all time. 'Mr Nicklaus,' said Jones, 'plays a game with which I am not familiar.'

His words summed up not only the best golf ever to have been seen at Augusta but it also reflected the considerable mark Nicklaus was already making in a still young professional career. It was only his fourth year on the US Tour and already he had won the Masters twice, in 1963 and now 1965, the US Open in 1962 and the US PGA in 1963. A year later, in 1966, he completed his first full set of the major championships by taking the British Open at Muirfield.

In the days of Jones, before the Masters had come into being, the Amateur Championships of America and Britain were counted as 'Majors', together with the two Opens. Jones was triumphant 13 times between 1923 and 1930 and then retired. Nicklaus, who before turning professional, took the US Amateur in 1959 and 1961, equalled that record with his third US Open at Pebble Beach in 1972. A year later, when he took the US PGA for a third time, he passed it and such has since been the enduring excellence of his game that he is unquestionably the most successful golfer of all time.

Yet in many ways there have been two Jack Nicklauses. The first was a raw and rather overweight college-type golfer known more for his sheer strength than any finesse. The final model bore little resemblance, the crew-cut gone and replaced by a fair, almost wavy and much more attractive hair-style. His weight also dropped from a peak of 215 lb (97.5 kg) to a low of 175 lb (79.4 kg). He was consequently 'a different man'.

Nicklaus admits in his autobiography that at his heaviest he was a much more powerful player, and his appearance, even to the extent of double chins, did not concern him. He changed his mind towards the end of the 1960s, however, and particularly after the 1969 Ryder Cup match at Royal Birkdale when 36 holes in a day began to tire him.

By then Nicklaus was established as the

world's supreme golfer. It had been no surprise. Even as an amateur he had, in 1960, been runner-up to Arnold Palmer in the US Open at Cherry Hills. It was in the same Championship, two years later at Oakmont, that he recorded his first victory as a professional. If that was not a phenomenal enough feat in itself, it was also achieved in a head-to-head confrontation with the great American hero of that time, Arnold Palmer, in a play-off.

It has often been said that Palmer ought to have won but did not because he kept taking three putts on the notoriously slick Oakmont greens which Sam Snead once compared to trying to stop a ball halfway down a marble staircase. Certainly Palmer did take three putts 13 times over the 90 holes whereas Nicklaus made only one such lapse. But this does not take into account the 25 occasions on which Palmer missed a green with his approach but still got down in two with the help of single putts.

An adoring American public was nevertheless shattered and they did not take kindly to this young upstart with his apparent disregard for a living legend. Even at Augusta, where the crowds are claimed to be the fairest in America, Nicklaus felt himself to be regarded as

Portrait of the early Jack Nicklaus.
Far left Jack Nicklaus crosses the Swilcan burn on his first visit to St Andrews for the 1964 Open.

Jack Nicklaus on the 18th green at Muirfield putting for his first Open title in 1966.

a sort of Black Knight whose mistakes were even cheered.

It is testimony to the character of the man therefore that he was gradually able to win the hearts of his critics as, time and time again, he reserved his best for the big occasion. In Britain he has always been a great favourite and just as Palmer led the annual American cavalcade to the Open, so too has Nicklaus remained its most loyal supporter, putting as he does the major championships before all else.

Unlike Palmer, who played by instinct and could never resist a challenging shot, Nicklaus was more of a golfing tactician. He showed that instinct when he won the British Open for the first time at Muirfield in 1966. The rough was 'elephant' high and Nicklaus virtually discarded his driver in favour of an iron from the tee. That would never have been in the nature of Palmer but, calculating though he may be, Nicklaus is also a sentimentalist. Muirfield had been the place where he first played in Britain, in the 1959 Walker Cup match, and when he came to build his first course in Ohio, he called it Muirfield Village.

It was in the 1969 Ryder Cup match at Royal Birkdale that Nicklaus endeared himself utterly to the British sporting public. Tony Jacklin was at that time the man of the moment having earlier that summer become the first Briton to win the Open Championship for 18 years. Fittingly the two were drawn to play each other in the final singles and they alone were left on the course with the two sides level, coming to the 18th.

Both had awkward second putts to hole for their fours on the final green but Nicklaus, playing first, got his in and immediately picked up Jacklin's marker conceding him the half and the one and only tied match. 'I did not think you would miss it, Tony', said Nicklaus, 'but I was not going to give you the chance, either.'

No-one therefore begrudged for one moment Nicklaus's second Open victory at St Andrews the following year, 1970. To win at golf's headquarters was among his dearest ambitions. He had to beat Doug Sanders in a play-off to do it and that he got his 'second chance' was due only to Sanders having missed a putt of not much more than a yard for outright victory on the 72nd green. When they played the hole again the following day, little still separating them, Nicklaus also produced a nice touch of theatre as he peeled off his pullover before

Charles Coody helps Jack Nicklaus into his fourth green jacket after he had won the 1972 Masters.

Team man Nicklaus takes advice from partner Tom Weiskopf during the 1973 Ryder Cup at Muirfield.

driving through the green more than 350 yards away.

That same year Nicklaus passed his first $1 million in prize-money, and it took him only three years and 11 months to accumulate his second million. By 1975 he had been leading money-winner seven times and won 68 tournaments. But already he was beginning to think of pacing himself and 'peaking' only for the Majors.

Business interests were accumulating and his approach became more that of some rich amateur who could play for enjoyment rather than need. Golf is, after all, only a game and this was something Nicklaus never forgot.

Loyal as the Americans have been to the Walker Cup, even they admitted that something had to be done after another landslide victory at Seattle in 1961. Great Britain and Ireland were defeated by 11-1, which equalled their worst-ever reverse in Chicago in 1928. Martin Christmas scored the only British point and there was not even a glimmer of a silver lining, so superior were the United States.

The 36-hole format, with four foursomes on the first day and eight singles on the second, was weighted in favour of the stronger team and, in an effort to redress the balance, it was decided in 1963 to play two series of foursomes and singles, each over 18 holes, therefore doubling the number of points at stake.

Turnberry was the venue and immediately the British responded, leading 7½-4½ at the end of the first day and conjuring visions of a repeat of their only victory at St Andrews in 1938. But the Americans, aided by a succession of British errors at the 16th hole where they kept hitting their second shots into the burn short of the green, turned the tables and won again, this time by 14-10. It was their 18th victory in 19 matches.

What happened next confounded all predictions. At Baltimore in 1965, under the captaincy of Joe Carr, the British played as they had never played before in the United States. They took the opening foursomes 2½-1½, the singles 6-2 and led 8½-3½ at the halfway point. The second series of foursomes seemed crucial but the British stood firm, shared them 2-2 and remained five points clear with only eight singles to come.

Far from that final afternoon becoming a joyous procession, it became in turn a nightmare and finally a great escape. Though Gordon Cosh soon got a firm hold on one of the two points Britain needed, those around him were on the receiving end of a typically fierce American counter-attack. Match after match was lost and suddenly it was not victory Britain faced but defeat. Their only hope was Clive Clark, but even he was two down with three to play.

The stigma of it was too awful to contemplate but Clark won the 16th with a birdie and when his opponent, Mark Hopkins, shanked at the next, a short hole, the prospect was all-square coming to the 18th. Instead Hopkins somehow got a three from out of the woods to keep his lead and, after chipping close

Joe Carr on his way to victory in the 1958 Amateur Championship at St Andrews.

at the last, it was the United States who were poised to celebrate victory. There was, however, one last twist as Clark, 35 feet away in two, sank his putt for a birdie to draw level and, at the very last gasp, earn a tied Walker Cup match. They do not come any closer than that.

Two more American victories were to follow, in 1967 and 1969, then in 1971 at St Andrews Britain's years of anguish at last came to an end. They won by 13-11 but many again were the agonies they suffered before they reached the promised land.

Their start was unprecedented: all four foursomes won and the Americans in appparent disarray. But not for long. Back they came to take the singles 6½-1½ for an overall lead of 6½-5½, and the chip Vinny Giles holed from off the road at the 17th against the British captain, Michael Bonallack, seemed for all the world to indicate that the gods had not changed their allegiance.

Then the following morning the Americans increased their lead by another point by taking the second series of foursomes 2½-1½, and with Lanny Wadkins getting the upper hand against Bonallack in the top singles in a game played at a rare pace, the rest seemed little more

Clive Clark, who earned a vital half at Baltimore in 1956.

Rival captains of 1971. Bill Campbell (far left), captain of the US team, and Michael Bonallack.

than a formality. But gradually, in the late afternoon sunlight, the tide began to turn. Warren Humphreys began holing long putt after long putt against a stunned Steve Melnyk, Hugh Stuart beat Vinny Giles, Charlie Green won, then Roddy Carr and then George Macgregor. At the bottom of the order Geoffrey Marks was down to Tom Kite but Dr David Marsh was one up after 16 holes against Bill Hyndman and it was on his shoulders ultimately that the destiny of the Walker Cup rested.

Marsh's second shot to the 17th, a three-iron from the very centre of the fairway, was one of the finest strokes of the decade, given the circumstances. It never wavered, found the middle of the green and when he got his half in four it meant that not only could he no longer lose but that Britain had won. It was a rare and emotional moment.

Afterwards Bonallack, in paying tribute to his team, said that 'it had won despite its captain' which was an oblique reference to his losing three of his four games. If anything, however, the team had won it *for* its captain, for this was the ultimate and fitting climax to one of the greatest careers in amateur golf.

Though a player of almost ugly style, Bonallack was a supreme competitor with a wonderful touch on and around the greens. He would seemingly half-top every putt as he crouched low over the ball but his sense of line and pace broke the hearts of many an opponent. He was also the most modest of men and a true sporting ambassador for Britain.

Through the 1960s he was totally dominant, winning both the British Amateur Championship and the English Amateur Championship five times each. His hat-trick of triumphs in the British, beginning in 1968, was unprecedented, while he also won the English Stroke-Play Championship four times, once tieing. Between 1957 and 1971 he took the Berkshire Trophy, another leading stroke-play event, five times outright and tied for it on another occasion. He was Essex Amateur Champion 11 times, made nine Walker Cup appearances, eight Eisenhower Trophy appearances and played for England for 16 consecutive years and 17 in all.

He always stressed the importance of a 'fast start', in other words playing the 1st hole well, and he never entered a match without some sort of 'swing thought' or gimmick. It helped him to concentrate.

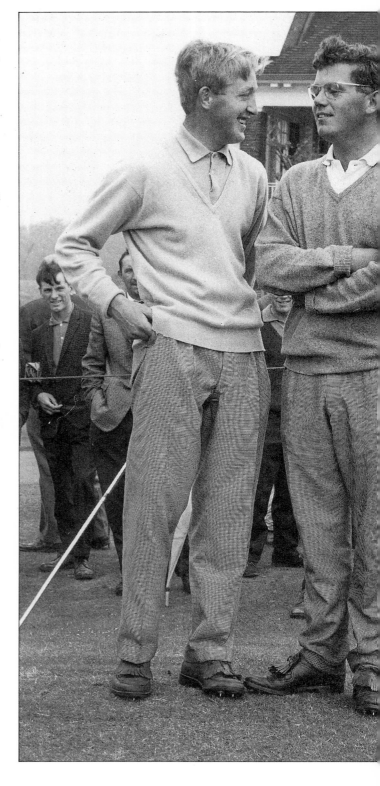

The youngest competitors in the Boys' Championship at Sunningdale in 1956. On the left, Malcolm Gregson (13), who later went on to become a successful professional, and on the right Rodney Foster (14) who was later to become a member of the winning Walker Cup team of 1971. Far left Rodney Foster (left) with David Marsh, to whom he was to lose in the final of the English Amateur Championship of 1964.

Jubilation for members of the 1971 Walker Cup team as David Marsh clinches a British victory. Left to right: Scott Macdonald, George Macgregor, Charlie Green, Hugh Stuart, Warren Humphreys, Roddy Carr.

Of all Bonallack's many achievements, perhaps the most celebrated came in 1968 when he won the last of his five English Amateur Championships, at Ganton, one of Britain's finest inland courses. David Kelley, his opponent, resolved beforehand to try and forget Bonallack and just play the course, in par if he could, which he did. Little good it did him, for though Kelley was round in an approximate 72 in the morning, he found himself 11 down. Bonallack, at his most undeniable, holed the course in 61 strokes and shortly after lunch won by 12 and 11, a record margin. There has been nothing like it, before or since.

The victor and the vanquished. Arnold Palmer was the winner of the first World Match-Play in 1964 and Neil Coles (below) his unfortunate opponent.

Mark McCormack's contribution to golf has not only been confined to making the stars of the game into multi-millionaires. In 1964 he came up with the idea of a world match-play championship. It was staged at Wentworth and Piccadilly were the sponsors and it immediately caught the imagination of the public. There was a ring to the name that identified it instantly with London Town, the autumn date was perfect for the climax to the British season and even to this day, under the banner now of changed sponsorship, there is a tendency to think of it as 'the Piccadilly'.

Early fields were limited to eight players, all straight out of the top drawer, the matches were played over 36 holes and altogether there was a style about it that has endured more lastingly than many innovations to the golfing calendar. At first players were put up in the best London hotels and spirited back and forth by limousine. Then, as the traffic worsened, they graduated to the big houses on the Wentworth estate with personal cooks and staff to attend to their every need.

Three of the world's major champions accepted invitations that first year. Arnold Palmer had won the Masters for a then-record fourth time, Ken Venturi the United States Open and Tony Lema the Open. The standard was set, the crowds flocked in and the climax could hardly have been better orchestrated as Palmer, whose star was then in the ascendancy, beat Neil Coles, one of two British players in the field, by 2 and 1 in the final.

If a 'good winner' was all the tournament needed to get it safely launched, there is equally no doubt that the most significant contribution was to come from Gary Player, not only because the little South African proved himself to be a master of match-play but because in 1965 he made a recovery the like of which has never been repeated.

Having disposed of Coles in the first round, Player met in the semi-finals Lema who, in the year before his tragic death in a plane crash, was very much a rising star; a true throughbred with a swing to match. They called him 'Champagne Tony' because of his habit of buying the Press champagne whenever he won.

Earlier that year Player had won his only US Open, at St Louis, to complete a full set of the major championships (British Open 1959,

Gary Player receives advice from fellow South African Harold Henning, who acted as caddie for him during the World Match-Play in 1964.

Masters 1961 and US PGA 1962) but dismissal from the Piccadilly seemed inevitable when he went into lunch against Lema six down. Then he lost the first hole in the afternoon as well and was therefore seven down with 17 to play.

Player, because of his size, has always had something to prove, in life perhaps as well as in golf. His contribution has been immense, his lasting qualities being illustrated by the fact that he won the Open Championship in three different decades, 1959–68–74, as well as being so dominant in America that, together with Arnold Palmer and Jack Nicklaus, he was known as one of The Big Three. As a South African who commuted again and again to the States, no-one has flown more miles in pursuit of his golf and Player's character in the face of anti-apartheid threats was always exemplary.

Such qualities were also invaluable on the golf course, particularly in that match against Lema. He was still five down with nine to play. But now the errors were more on Lema's side as he lost the two short holes, and the 10th and 14th, to pars, the 11th to a birdie and the 16th to another par, though in fact it was never needed because Lema was in so much trouble that he conceded. It reduced the margin between them

Tony Lema, who was unlucky to be on the receiving end of Gary Player's great fightback in 1965.

to a single hole with two to play. The 17th they halved in birdie fours, Player got another at the 18th to square and a four at the first extra hole, their 37th of the day, completed an heroic recovery.

Having made good his escape, Player went on to win the first of his five World Match-Plays, defeating the reigning Open Champion, Peter Thomson, in the final. A year later he made a successful defence of the title, beating Jack Nicklaus in the final, though it was not so much this as the controversy that attended the final that hit the headlines.

The rule book, it is said, is there to help and not hinder and it is advisable for every professional to have a thorough knowledge of the rules just in case he leaves himself under unnecessary disadvantage. Nicklaus, more than most, has been aware of this and when, at the 9th hole in the morning he hooked his drive, he found so savage a place in the deep rough that he knew at once that he had little chance of reaching the green. However his keen eye also observed an advertising board situated some way away but nevertheless in a direct line between him and the green.

As relief can be given for such artificial obstructions, Nicklaus asked Colonel Tony Duncan, the referee, for a free drop but it was Duncan's opinion that the sign was so far away that it could not possibly interfere with Nicklaus's shot, bearing in mind the lie. He refused the request. Nicklaus, one down at the time, took the decision with a rare display of bad grace, conceded the hole and was so clearly upset that Duncan asked him if he would like another referee, which might not altogether have been the wisest thing to do since it could have been interpreted that he might have been in the wrong. Few witnesses would have agreed but Nicklaus accepted the offer and the duties were taken over by Gerald Micklem, an acknowledged authority on the rules.

Nicklaus in fact won the next two holes with birdies which suggested that he quickly got over the incident. But he went into lunch four down and Player beat him in the end by the comfortable margin of 6 and 4. In due course Nicklaus came to regret his behaviour but it was nevertheless four years before he came back, defeating Lee Trevino in the 1970 final.

There were in the late 1960s some lovely days of autumn sunshine for the Match-Play, memories of ochre leaves, stretching shadows, glistening dew and Bob Charles, the only left-hander ever to have won a major championship (the Open in 1963) holing putts all over Wentworth as first he lost to Player in the 1968 final and then, a year later, going one better

Gary Player wearing a
blazer which endorsed his
supremacy in match-play
golf.

World Match-Play opponents: all four had their year of success. Right Hale Irwin and Graham Marsh at Wentworth in 1975. Far right David Graham congratulates Isao Aoki after he had holed in one at the 2nd in 1979 to win a holiday home in Scotland.

as he beat Gene Littler at the 37th, the first final to go into extra holes.

Every year, almost without fail, some sterling match would develop over the Burma Road, as the West course is also known, high among its classics being that thrilling confrontation in the 1972 semi-finals when Tony Jacklin came from four down almost to catch Lee Trevino. It may so have exhausted the Mexican that in the final he went down to Tom Weiskopf, who a year later was to win the Open.

It was nevertheless turning into something of a benefit event for the little man in black, Player. He won for a fourth time in 1973, but so protracted was the final that it very nearly had to be carried over into an extra day. Darkness was fast enveloping the course when Player at last prevailed at the 40th against Graham Marsh of Australia, who at two down with four to play, took three holes in a row to lead as they came to the 18th. Match-play, and particularly the World Match-play, always manages to throw up such moments.

Just as Arnold Palmer was responsible for the golfing boom in America, so it was Tony Jacklin who fired the enthusiasm in Britain. Though of humble origins, his father driving a locomotive in a Scunthorpe steelworks, he was born to be a star. He had an instant appeal that stretched far beyond the limited boundaries of golf, reaching out to people who scarcely knew the meaning of words like pars and birdies.

Jacklin has been without question Britain's most successful and famous golfer since the Second World War and in the late Sixties and early Seventies he was ranked among the best players in the world. In 1969 he became the first British golfer to win the Open Championship in 18 years – an unprecedentedly long interval – and within a year he had added to it the United States Open Championship, which made him the first man from the European side of the Atlantic to win the two titles since Ted Ray (British Open 1912, US Open 1920).

With any sort of luck Jacklin's achievements would have been even more encompassing but his failures were as spectacular as his successes for he was the sort of man to whom things simply 'happened'. He gave golf in Britain a new belief in itself and it was through him that the game in Europe stands in the position it does today.

None of it was done without a lot of hard work, however. His amateur career was just long enough for him to be capped by England Boys and his good fortune on turning professional in 1961 at the age of 17 was that he came under the care of Bill Shankland at Potters Bar. Shankland drove his assistants hard but it proved a most worthwhile training ground when, within three years, Jacklin turned his attention to the tournament circuits.

A winter in South Africa was followed by an invitation to his first tournament in America for the Carling Tournament, and when he came home he promptly won the Assistants' Championship, a small but important step towards the international arena that was his ambition.

By the end of 1966 Jacklin had played for England in the World Cup and in the spring of the following year he not only received his first invitation to play in the Masters at Augusta National but, in one round, outscored his partner, Arnold Palmer. This was to Jacklin an

The final putt drops and Tony Jacklin is the Open Champion of 1969.

indication that one day he could beat the rest of the world and from that moment his career took off.

He won two tournaments in 1967, the Pringle and the Dunlop Masters, but it was his victory in the latter at Royal St George's that indicated that somehow he was 'something special'. Not only did he have a final round of 64 but it included a hole-in-one at the 16th, the first time such a feat had been done in front of the telivision cameras.

This brought golf, and Jacklin, into every living-room in the land and his name was on everyone's lips again when in 1968 he returned to America and won the Jacksonville Tournament against the might of the US Tour. Now Britain really did have someone who could win the Open and in 1969, at Royal Lytham, the long years of suffering at the hands of the visitors from overseas came to an end.

From the start Jacklin was in the thick of things, a 68 in the first round, a 70 in the second and three strokes behind Bob Charles. But on the third day Jacklin returned a 70, the New Zealander a 75 and that three-stroke defecit had become a two-stroke advantage. A nation held its breath and its people were not

Aspiring champions David Butler, Sean Hunt and Tony Jacklin at the Assistants' Championship at Hartsbourne in 1965.

Tony Jacklin strides ahead
of his partner Peter
Townsend during the 1969
Ryder Cup. Jacklin was
unbeaten in his six matches.

Tony Jacklin, his wife
Vivien and son Bradley
arrive home with the US
Open trophy in 1970.

A recording session for Tony Jacklin in 1970. Such was his popularity that the offers kept flooding in.

disappointed. The memory now is of Jacklin playing any number of exquisite bunker shots when his lead was in danger of crumbling and then his final moment of glory, still two ahead and one hole to play.

The drive at the 18th at Lytham is not the easiest across a diagonal line of bunkers but Jacklin who, at this time in his career, had a wonderful rhythm, could not have hit a better stroke, piercing the very centre of the fairway and far beyond the bunkers. A few minutes later he had played a comfortable 7-iron to the centre of the green, safely got his four and received a salute that brought many a tear to the eye.

There was similar emotion later that season when Great Britain and Ireland, as the team was then composed, held the United States to a tie in the Ryder Cup match at Royal Birkdale. Inevitably Jacklin was again in the thick of it, winning two foursomes with Peter Townsend and then contributing another one and a half points in the fourball play with Neil Coles. Even so the two sides were still level after two days at 8–8.

At that time 16 singles were played on the last day, eight in the morning and another eight in the afternoon, and team captain Eric Brown played Jacklin last each time, sensing a close finish. Sam Snead, Brown's opposite number, was of like mind and put Jack Nicklaus as his anchor man.

Thus the stage was set for a gripping struggle as first Britain forged ahead by taking the morning singles 5–3 with Jacklin defeating Nicklaus by 4 and 3. But the Americans came back at them after lunch and the two sides were still level with only Jacklin and Nicklaus still on the course.

The penultimate singles saw Brian Huggett hole the bravest of putts on the last green to halve with Billy Casper and he broke down in tears believing that at that moment Britain had won. Seconds earlier he had heard a thunderous cheer from the direction of the 17th and he interpreted it as Jacklin again having beaten Nicklaus. It was not so.

The eagle putt Jacklin holed was to draw level and everything therefore hinged on the last hole. Very properly they halved that as well, Nicklaus making the supreme gesture by not asking Jacklin to hole a second putt that might just have been long enough to have been missed. But Jacklin, the Open Champion, had played a massive part in the one and only tied

Ryder Cup match.

Yet the most staggering achievement was the manner of Jacklin's victory the following year in the US Open at Hazeltine in Minnesota. On a course that by and large drove the Americans to despair, with Palmer taking 79 in the first round and Jack Nicklaus 81 in a difficult wind, Jacklin began with a 71 and led from start to finish. His subsequent scores were 70 in each round and he won in a canter, seven strokes clear of Dave Hill.

Only a few weeks later Jacklin began his defence of his British Open title at St Andrews with an outward half of 29 and then started for home with another birdie. No-one knows what might have happened had not a violent storm broken over the Old Course half an hour or so later. Jacklin was playing the 14th and had just hit his second shot into a bush when the heavens opened and washed out play for the day. Jacklin had all night to contemplate his next move but, when it came, the magic was gone. He finished the round in 67 and in the end had to settle for fifth place, three strokes behind Nicklaus and Doug Sanders, who tied before Nicklaus won the play-off.

A year later, in 1971, Jacklin was third behind Lee Trevino at Royal Birkdale, but opportunity beckoned once more at Muirfield in 1972 when he was locked in a historic and agonizing struggle with Trevino. Twice the title had looked Jacklin's for the taking; first in the third round until the Mexican edged past him with five birdies in the last five holes as he twice holed from off the green, and then late on the final day.

There was nothing between them coming to the 17th but when Trevino drove into a bunker and could only just get out, he went so far as to say: 'It's all yours, Tony.' But it was not. With one last despairing throw of the dice, Trevino chipped from the back of the green for his five whereas Jacklin, just short in two, chipped weakly and then took three putts for a six. Trevino needed no further bidding. His four at the last to Jacklin's five was decisive and indeed it was Nicklaus, after a last glorious round of 66, who was runner-up.

Nor was this the only time Trevino thwarted Jacklin. Later that same year they met in the semi-finals of the World Match-Play at Wentworth and it was Trevino who made all the early running, four up at lunch. There followed a stirring recovery as Jacklin went out in the afternoon in 29 to lead one up. With one hole to play they were level but it was Trevino who got the decisive birdie to win one up. Jacklin was nevertheless round in 63 and had lost with honour.

Despite this score something snapped

Tony Jacklin nearly regained his Open title at Royal Birkdale in 1971 and (below) went close again after an epic struggle with Lee Trevino at Muirfield in 1972.

within Jacklin that autumn day. He did not threaten in a major championship again. A man of considerable wealth, he temporarily seemed to lose the desire and, when he tried to come back, those deep reserves within him were drained.

His putting touch deserted him and the strain it put on the rest of his game found further weaknesses. Little things, like the click of a camera, distracted him more and more and the golden years became a memory, glorious though they were.

Henry Longhurst playing in the Worplesdon Mixed Foursomes in 1946.

Each autumn the Association of Golf Writers, a British collection of journalists now joined by some of their more distinguished colleagues from overseas, has to nominate the winner of the Golf Writer's Trophy. 'It shall,' according to the constitution, 'be awarded each year to the individual man or woman, born and resident in Europe who, in the opinion of the majority of members, shall have done the most for European golf during the preceding 12 months.' Originally one would have read 'Britain' instead of 'Europe' but the expansion of golf this side of the Atlantic onto the continent led to a wider area of selection.

The award does not necessarily go to an individual. In 1964 it was awarded to the Great Britain and Ireland Eisenhower Trophy team, which had won in Rome; in 1971 it went to the triumphant Walker Cup team and occasionally it has also gone to administrators like Gerald Micklem and even the Golf Foundation, which looks after the development of the game at junior level.

For some years it was also keenly debated over a succession of dinner tables on the tour whether the award should not go to one of its own members, Henry Longhurst, first and foremost a writer but also one of the most loved broadcasters in the game. He was in on the ground floor of televised golf, just as he had also been one of the pioneers of outside broadcasts for radio, and his distinctive voice and masterly turn of phrase made a significant contribution to the popularity of golf, particularly in Britain but also in America.

Longhurst was, in his younger days, a more than useful golfer. He was a Cambridge Blue and good enough, in 1936, to win the German Amateur Championship. But he was also a man of many parts, his motto in life being that everything was worth doing once. He was a Member of Parliament for Acton and once wrote a book on oil, which contained a Foreword by no less a person than Winston Churchill.

The ease of his writing was a delight and he contributed a regular column in *The Sunday Times* for 21 years without missing a single issue. It was compulsive reading for every golfer, being, Longhurst once dryly observed, 'just the right length for the smallest room in the house after breakfast before setting out for the links'.

NOT TRANSFERABLE

ACTON DIVISION of THE COUNTY of MIDDLESEX

PARLIAMENTARY ELECTION

Admit *Capt H. C. Longhurst*

to the Counting of Votes

in the Central Hall, Acton Lane, Acton

on 15th DECEMBER, 1943, at 10.30 a.m.

H. C. LOCKYER,
Deputy Acting Returning Officer.

The Declaration of Secrecy must also be produced.

Television nevertheless provided him with a whole new audience and it was his experience of playing the game at a quite high level that was one of his strengths. He was able to recognize what was going on in a player's mind in moments of crisis. This was well illustrated at the Open Championship at St Andrews in 1970 when, on the 72nd green, Doug Sanders faced a putt of around a yard to beat Jack Nicklaus by a stroke. Longhurst knew how missable it was in such circumstances and his quiet 'Oh, dear' when Sanders, having apparently settled himself, suddenly bent to remove some imaginary or, at the most, stray

Henry Longhurst commentating for television at the Daks Tournament at Wentworth in 1957.

strand of grass between his ball and the hole; to Longhurst it foretold the break in concentration that could only result in the putt being missed. It was and Nicklaus won the play-off.

Unlike radio, where the commentator has to keep talking, television, with a picture there all the time for the viewer, also gave Longhurst the opportunity to make full use of what he called his 'brilliant flashes of silence'. He would keep his mouth shut when a player was hitting to the green or putting and, if he missed a putt that ought to have been holed, Longhurst would sum it up with something like: 'Well, there's not much more we can say about that.'

It was in 1965, on a visit to America, that Longhurst was invited one day to go up one of the towers and see for himself how television worked in the States. While there he spoke only a few words but they were enough for a CBS producer, Frank Chirkinian, to recognize that he had made a 'find'. Longhurst was promptly invited back to take care of the 16th hole at the Masters and he also became a member of the ABC team at such events as the US Open and PGA Championships. The making of him, he recalls in his autobiography, *My Life and Soft Times*, was when he described a terrible shot by

143

Leonard Crawley, a great sportsman and writer.
Far right Bernard Darwin, possibly the greatest golf writer of all time, with the President's Putter in 1930.

Homero Blancas as 'a terrible shot'. Such honesty was unheard-of and the Americans lapped him up.

As a raconteur he was without peer and he was much in demand as an after-dinner speaker. He was also brave enough to admit, in print, in 1973, the time he felt it prudent to take his own life. Fortunately it was one of the few jobs he botched.

An 'awareness' in the lower abdomen revealed a tumour and that in turn meant a colostomy and, as he described it, 'removal of part of the colon, and furthermore, if you will forgive me, an artificial orifice in the side of the body'. It was that which decided him.

'I enquired of three doctors (not of course including my own)' he wrote, 'as to whether I had obtained sufficient pills to exercise man's inalienable right, as Hamlet put it, to "shuffle off this mortal coil", and all said yes – one recommending rather splendidly, "half a bottle of whisky and make sure they don't find you for 12 hours".'

It so happened that Longhurst had previously been presented with a bottle of Glenmorangie malt whisky. 'The fatal night,' he then recalls, 'with my mind still made up, called clearly for a bottle of this powerful nectar with which to slide peacefully away and I attacked it with maudlin vigour, but alas, or rather hooray,

I must have exceeded the stated dose and Glenmorangie got the better of me before I got round to taking the pills.'

Longhurst was one of the first British writers each year to visit the Masters and his vivid accounts of the tournament's colourful setting were instrumental in giving it the major status it has today. Other prominent writers such as Pat Ward-Thomas, Leonard Crawley and Peter Ryde soon followed in his wake and their descriptions of the then-revolutionary scoring system, which was related by a player's progress against par (0, 0, -1, -2, -1, and so on), set a fashion that has since been copied worldwide.

By the early Seventies the European Tour was in its infancy but year by year it grew, attracting not only bigger and better fields but a bigger and bigger caravan of attendant writers. Conditions were often spartan, Press rooms in tiny rooms high in the eaves of clubhouses with telephones that seldom worked. Scores would be delivered by a shopping basket attached to a rope and the nearest you got to a leaderboard would be a piece of paper stuck to a tree by a drawing-pin.

Again, however, the American way of life set the style. First in Britain and then on the Continent, efficiently-run Press rooms with telephones that really did work took over, as did

The Press room at a modern Open Championship.

Henry Longhurst's successors at the BBC. Left to right: Bruce Critchley, Clive Clark, Peter Alliss, Alex Hay and Harry Carpenter.

the interview area. Any player with a potentially leading or closely challenging score would be whisked in for a de-briefing and the task of the writer was much eased by a blow-by-blow account of his round.

The Press marquees are now among the biggest at the major championships, often air-conditioned in the heat of an American summer and, while tournament golf would be nothing without the quality of its players, it is also dependent on writers and broadcasters to describe it.

RING OUT THE OLD 1.62, RING IN THE NEW 1.68

By **MICHAEL McDONNELL**

THE traditional British golf ball will soon become a collector's item.

It is to be scrapped within three years.

The decision means that the few remaining enthusiasts will have to get rid of their existing stocks before January, 1990 when the 1.62 inch diameter golf ball becomes illegal.

Britain and the rest of the world are to fall into line and use the American size 1.68 inch diameter golf ball at all levels of the game.

Theory

It is already compulsory in all European tour events and championships.

The Royal & Ancient Golf Club of St Andrews, the sport's governing body, announced the change yesterday, although the small ball was virtually extinct anyway.

More than 12 million golf balls are sold annually in Britain but demand for the small size has been so poor that Dunlop stopped production almost four years ago.

A survey showed that only five per cent of golfers steadfastly refused to use the new ball.

A Dunlop spokesman said : 'The old theory was that the smaller ball went further and that the bigger ball ballooned in the wind.'

The Daily Mail *announces the last rites.*

British professional golf underwent two important changes in the late Sixties and early Seventies. Tony Jacklin was on the march and the tournament circuit was beginning to grow. No longer were the players dividing their time, as did their predecessors, between the professional's shop and the occasional tournament. They became a different breed of men, playing competitively week after week and having very different interests to the other half of their profession, whose main concern still was with their club members, selling equipment and

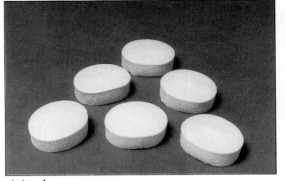

giving lessons.

Because of this the tournament stars wanted a greater say in their affairs and there followed an at times bitter wrangle as they sought to break away from their parent body, the Professional Golfers' Association, to set up their own Tournament Players' Division.

The man at the centre of the storm was John Jacobs, who by 1971 had become the first Tournament Director-General and was able, at the end of that year, to announce that the following season prize-money would be doubled to the best part of £½ million. This proved to be the breakthrough for from that point the tournament players, represented then by the Tournament Players' Division, and the club players, represented still by the PGA, began more and more to go their separate ways.

In those days the Tournament Players' Division offices were in a small back room of the Oval cricket ground – a far cry from the PGA European Tour's present opulent headquarters at Wentworth – but for all their small size they were a focal point for much political manoeuvring and discussion. Among other matters there was wide concern that the standard of play in Britain had fallen further behind that

of the Americans than it should have done. Climate, the sheer weight of numbers and superior putting were all at various times listed as the reasons. But there was also an enlightened if small school of thought which held the opinion that the British were on the wrong track in their persistent use of the 1.62 in (41 mm) ball. It was known as the 'small ball' as against the larger 1.68 in (43 mm) ball the Americans played.

It certainly made little sense that the same game should be played with golf balls of different size and Tony Jacklin, who at least had first-hand and current experience of playing in

America, was a strong advocate of the bigger ball. Though harder to control, especially in a wind, the belief was that, once mastered, it produced a better and more complete player.

Accordingly it was tried for an experimental three-year period in 1968 in all professional tournaments. Jacklin's victories in the Open Championship of 1969 and the US Open of 1970 strengthened the arm of the big-ball lobbyists though during this period both the Royal and Ancient and the United States Golf Association, who were beginning to work together towards a standardization of the Rules of Golf, were making statements that they were trying to produce a uniform ball of an entirely different size.

They had in mind a ball of 1.66 in (42 mm) diameter, though whether such a specific was by design or accident remains a matter of some doubt. At all events it would have a velocity restriction of 255 feet per second (78 metres per second), which was the same as the big ball. There was no velocity restriction on the small ball.

By 1972 the R & A had arranged extensive tests with the 1.66 in (42 mm) ball in Australia, Canada, New Zealand, South Africa and Japan and had come to the conclusion that there was not only an 'overwhelming desire for a uniform ball' but that 'the 1.66 is suitable for play in these countries', according to an official statement from St Andrews.

The British PGA had meanwhile voted by a fairly narrow majority – but by a significantly larger majority among the top players, of whom Jacklin was of course one – to extend the 1.68 in (43 mm) ball experiment for another three years. This was much to the chagrin of the Golf Ball Manufacturers of London. They had a worldwide monopoly of the small-ball market and did not want to lose it.

There was also the not inconsiderable matter of having to change all their machinery, a very costly matter in itself.

Furthermore, they produced figures which revealed that, for all the insistence of the leading players, sales of the big ball were very limited – 6.2 per cent in 1968, 3.1 in 1969, 2.7 in 1970 and 1.7 in 1971. 'The mass of golfers,' stated the manufacturers, 'has clearly indicated its desire for the existing 1.62 inch ball.'

The manufacturers also forecast little support for the proposed 1.66 in (42 mm) ball either and by 1973 the R & A were beginning to admit that the prospects of an alternative ball ever coming onto the market were becoming slim. The USGA had told them that they were no longer interested, influenced as they were by a report from the American Ball Manufacturers, who had expressed 'serious reservations about the flight and other characteristics of the 1.66 ball'.

By April 1974 the R & A finally had to write and tell their 56 affiliated Unions and Associations that the uniform ball project had been abandoned and instead they dropped the bombshell that in that year's Open championship at Royal Lytham the 1.68 in (43

mm) ball would become mandatory. The Golf Ball Manufacturers Conference promptly sent a stinging letter to St Andrews expressing their 'surprise and anxiety'. They called it 'a most undesirable precedent', arguing that it 'destroyed the distinctive character imparted by playing the British ball under British conditions'.

The final paragraph stated: 'By adopting the 1.68 inch ball exclusively for the British Open, we feel that the R & A has first opened the door to the universal adoption of this ball. Secondly, and more important, the other tournament organizers will undoubtedly follow suit so that within the near future every golf

event of any importance will be played to American rules, and in consequence the standing and authority of our British governing body must inevitably and quite swiftly decline to that of simply one more National Golf Union. The dangers and disadvantages of this decision are, frankly, almost incalculable.'

The first part of this statement had a more prophetic ring to it than the second. Swiftly the big ball took hold, for the young were certainly not going to play with anything different to that used by the professionals. Furthermore the manufacturers, driven now into a corner, got their heads down and produced a 1.68 ball every bit as good as those in America. But it was a bitter feud while it lasted.

Eight stages in the manufacture of a modern golf ball.

Right *Babe Zaharias during the Ladies' Championship at Gullane, which she won in 1947. Below Angela Bonallack (right) with Curtis Cup partner Elizabeth Price. Below right Betsy Rawls, one of the pioneers of the US Ladies' Professional Golf Association.*

omen's golf in Britain was sleeping peacefully. The surge the game had enjoyed in the Fifties, with two Curtis Cup victories and then a tied match in America, had largely dissipated. The names of Marley Spearman and Angela Bonallack, wife of Michael, made forceful appearances on various honours boards but the image of twin set and tweed skirt prevailed. Professionalism was something to do with men, not women.

In America it was different. The LPGA (Ladies Professional Golfers' Association) Tour had been pottering along through the Fifties, gaining identity through the likes of the now legendary Babe Zaharias, Peggy Kirk, Louise Suggs, Marilyn Smith and Betsey Rawls. 'But you could not make money,' said Miss Rawls. 'We practically had to beg people to turn professional. If you played pro golf then, you really loved the game.'

It was with the arrival of Mickey Wright that the corner was turned in the early Sixties. Between 1961 and 1964 Miss Wright was the utterly dominant figure, winning 45 tournaments and being leading money-winner in each of those years. 'Mickey got the outside

A great spectator sport.
Above *Rain imminent at Sandwich during the 1981 Open at Royal St George's.*
Left *Umbrellas and anoraks at Royal Lytham for the 1979 Open.*
Far left *Suntans and shirtsleeves at Fulford in 1984.*

Above *Sizzling temperatures at Shinnecock Hills for the 1986 US Open.*
Left *Augusta in the rain, 1979.*

149

Golf – the great leveller. Even the best players occasionally hit a ball off line or miss a simple putt.
Right Greg Norman.
Far right Bernhard Langer.
Centre Craig Stadler.
Bottom left Seve Ballesteros.
Bottom right Graham Marsh.

Left and far left *More trouble for Philip Parkin and Tony Jacklin.*

Left *Nick Faldo struggles with a bad lie.*
Far left *The message that says it all. An unattended bag during the European Tour qualifying competition at La Manga.*

The caddies – great characters in vital supporting roles.
Right 'Irish' sports some original headgear.
Far right Nick de Paul practises some words of advice for Seve Ballesteros.

Right Distinctive caddie overalls for the Masters at Augusta.
Far right 'Mullins' – one of the old school.
Below Suitable dress at St Andrews for Magnus Persson's caddie at the 1984 Open.
Below right Hippy-style accompaniment on the US circuit.

world to take a second look at women golfers', Judy Rankin once remarked, 'and when they looked, they discovered the rest of us.'

By 1963 television began to take an interest and covered live the final round of the American Women's Open. It was an immediate success and by the end of the decade women's golf was quite regularly on the screen, prize-money having also been tripled to $600,000 in a programme of 34 events. The prolific Mickey Wright was succeeded by the even more prolific Kathy Whitworth, whose 88 victories remain a record for the LPGA. It was a colourful world, too, all pastel shades and bronzed limbs, but a tough environment even so.

For an amateur to invade and then conquer was unthinkable. But this was what a young French girl, Catherine Lacoste, managed to do when in 1967 she became not only the youngest winner, at 22, of the US Women's Open at Hot Springs, Virginia, but also the first amateur and the first overseas player. It was an historic moment, but then it could be said that Miss Lacoste had been born to be a champion.

Her father, René Lacoste, was a famous French lawn tennis player, winning the men's singles title at Wimbledon twice, in 1925 and 1928. Her mother, as Miss Thion de la Chaume, was the golfer. She won the British Championship in 1927. Such parental skills were bound to breed instinct for games. It was in the blood, and Catherine inherited it.

The signs were there early. Already junior champion of France, Miss Lacoste came to international prominence when in 1964 she led her country to victory in the inaugural Espirito Santo trophy, the Women's World Team Championship. It was played at St Germain on the outskirts of Paris and Catherine, then only 19, furthermore tied for the individual award alongside Carol Sorenson, who had just won the British Championship. In subsequent years, before her retirement in 1970, Miss Lacoste was twice third in the indvidual section of the World Team Championship and won it once, in 1968.

Blessed with a natural swing, Catherine learned her golf at Chantaco. That fine French golfer, Jean Garaialde, helped to apply the final touches and an exceptional talent was further revealed when in 1966 she came to Britain and won the Astor Salver at Prince's, Sandwich, with a remarkable 66 over a long and difficult course.

At a time when French women's golf

Catherine Lacoste takes on Gary Player in a friendly challenge match at Wentworth in 1969.
Left Carol Sorenson who tied with Catherine Lacoste for the individual title at the Women's World Team Championship in 1964.

153

Shelley Hamlin, the last hurdle for Catherine Lacoste before she completed her Grand Slam with the US Amateur title in 1969.

was rich with talent, Miss Lacoste's decision to play in the US Open in 1967 bore a touch of defiance since it coincided with the European Championship. No-one considered her seriously beforehand but an opening round of 71 launched her promisingly, just a stroke behind Sandra Haynie. When she followed it with a 70 on the second day, the French girl found herself clear of the field.

This she maintained through the third round but in the fourth her game fell away and she was severely threatened by Louise Suggs who, nine strokes behind with 18 holes to play, made up eight of them with only three to play. However Miss Lacoste took a grip on herself, and with a birdie at the 17th and a par three at the last, salvaged a final round of 79 to win by two strokes from Susie Maxwell and Beth Stone, Miss Suggs having come to grief at the 16th.

Against the then cream of the American professional tour, it was an extraordinary performance, but Catherine's abiding ambition was to win the British Championship, as her mother had done. For some time it was frustrated but in 1969 the Championship was held in Northern Ireland, at Royal Portrush, not too far from the scene of her mother's triumph at Royal County Down, the other side of Belfast. Such was her diligence that she arrived a week early and, watched by her mother, practised until she knew the course by heart. Slowly she worked her way through to the final where she met and was in danger of losing to Ann Irvin. Four down at one point, Miss Lacoste inched her way back and won on the last green.

Already that year Catherine had taken the French and Spanish Championships and it was natural for her to go for the last leg of the Grand Slam, the US Amateur Championship at Las Colinas in Texas. It was nevertheless not an easy decision for there was now the additional strain of being 'expected to win' every time she went out. Furthermore there are cooler places in the world than Texas in August.

However, once committed, she defeated Polly Riley in the first round, Constance Hirschman in the second and Mary Jane Fassinger in the third. Only one of these matches was close, but in the semi-finals Catherine faced Anne Welts (née Quast and now Sander) and stood three down after 10 holes. But, as in the British event, she rallied splendidly to win by 2 and 1.

Just one step now remained for golfing immortality and Catherine had to be at her best to resist Shelley Hamlin in the final. Three up after nine of the 36 holes, the French girl had to resist a spirited recovery as Miss Hamlin played the next 25 holes in level par. Others might have wilted, but Miss Lacoste did not and she was still three up when she won on the 34th green.

A year later Catherine Lacoste married and effectively retired from competitive golf. She did however make one more appearance in the World Team Championship in Madrid, her Spanish husband's native city, but the competitive edge had gone and, in a gripping finish, it was the Americans who just got the better of the French.

As a driver and long-iron player, Miss Lacoste was the best since Babe Zaharias. There was a boldness about her that set her apart but it was the blood of champions already in her veins that, in a sense, made it more inevitable than in most.

PART FIVE

THE MODERN GAME,
FROM 1975 ONWARDS

Tony Jacklin acts as chauffeur for Bernhard Langer, Seve Ballesteros, Nick Faldo and Vivien Jacklin at PGA National during the 1983 Ryder Cup.
Far right The Great Britain & Europe team for the 1985 Ryder Cup, lined up in their wet weather uniform.

Novel location for a scoreboard at PGA National.
Far right Hal Sutton (extreme left) and Craig Stadler hardly seem inclined to shake hands after only managing a tie with Bernhard Langer and Jose-Maria Canizares in their fourball on the first day of the Ryder Cup in 1985.

The opening ceremony for the 1985 Ryder Cup at The Belfry.
Far right Tony Jacklin with mini television in hand, shares the strain of captaincy with his opposite number, Lee Trevino.

As proud words go, none have rung out more resoundingly than Tony Jacklin's around the amphitheatre of the 18th green at The Belfry, near Sutton Coldfield. Europe had just won the Ryder Cup; Concorde had roared over this peaceful patch of Warwickshire countryside dipping its wings in salute and Jacklin was reintroducing his team to an ecstatic crowd. He did it soccer-style, name by name, title by title, and the thousands around the clubhouse just roared and roared. 'Ladies and Gentlemen,' said Jacklin, 'Open Champion, Sandy Lyle.' Lyle stepped forward a pace and grinned. 'Masters Champion, Bernhard Langer.' Langer did likewise. 'The best player in the world, Seve Ballesteros,' and the Spaniard acknowledged the tribute and the occasion with his widest smile and by waving both arms.

Moment earlier Seve had given his verdict on the events of 15 September 1985. 'It is just fantastic,' he said. 'It is like winning another Open,' and for Ballesteros, there can be no higher praise.

It was not a unique occasion, for the Americans have been beaten four times since the 1920s when the Ryder Cup matches started. But this *was* the first time that a team labelled Europe had won and it set a magnificent seal on a year in European golf in which a great many dreams had come true. Langer had not only won the Masters, he won the Heritage Classic the following week and established himself as the next best player in the world to Ballesteros. Then Lyle fulfilled an occasionally erratic talent by taking the Open Championship at Royal St George's, Sandwich, to make himself the world number three. Although Ballesteros missed out narrowly on the Majors, he still won five times in Europe, and so a Spaniard, a West German and a Briton – above all, three Europeans – headed the world rankings. It was, for many people, an almost unbelievable situation.

There were many reasons for it. The adoption of the bigger ball meant that players had to find a better way of hitting it, for the small British ball was much more forgiving and a whole generation had, by 1985, grown up without ever relying on the 1.62 version rather than the 1.68.

There was also the vastly increased competition in Europe as a new breed of professional golfer began to emerge, who did nothing but play in tournaments. Indeed most of

the top players had begun to travel all round the world, literally, in search of success and it was perhaps only in 1983 when Europe lost by only one point in America that a team which was as battle-hardened as the Americans finally surfaced. Then there was the happy coincidence that three indisputably world-class players in Ballesteros, Langer and Lyle all arrived on the scene at roughly the same time. Young, dedicated and hugely talented, they were probably the three best players at The Belfry on either side and quite apart from their contribution to the points total, their presence and their achievements helped to lift the remainder of the team.

Others in the team had some claim to world status but had yet to prove it in a major championship. Sam Torrance who, moist-eyed though he was, could still see well enough to hole the final 15-footer for the birdie at the 18th that beat Andy North and won the Ryder Cup; Howard Clark, who was to go on and win the individual section of the World Cup, and Ian Woosnam who in July 1986 was to walk under the winds of Turnberry to finish third in the Open to Greg Norman.

They played a huge part in it all, as did the Spanish Armada that sailed forth on the afternoon of the second day and totally routed the opposition. Not one of the four men would have been eligible until 1979 but now Captain Jacklin gave them the responsibility to go out and win, and in so doing, they established a lead that the Americans would not be able to overtake on the final day. First out that afternoon were Jose-Maria Canizares and Jose Rivero, who destroyed Tom Kite and Calvin Peete by 7 and 5. Then Ballesteros and Manuel Pinero crushed Craig Stadler and Hal Sutton 5 and 4 and when at the end of the day Europe had established a 9–7 lead it was the first time since 1949 that America had been second going into the final day.

One of the reasons for that lead lay in what happened on the 18th green on the morning of the second day. Lyle and Langer, two down with two to play against Curtis Strange and Craig Stadler, won the 17th when Lyle holed a 45-footer for an eagle. But both Europeans missed birdie putts on the last and eventually Stadler was left with a putt of no more than 14 inches for a one-hole win. In any circumstances other than the one pertaining, i.e. the most important team event in golf, the putt

The agony of Craig Stadler after his missed putt at the final hole on the second morning at The Belfry.

Elation for Tony Jacklin as another putt drops for his side.

would have been a gimme, but quite correctly Stadler was asked to tap it in. As he shaped to do so the voice of Bruce Critchley, the television commentator, intoned the fateful words: 'That's a certain four' and suddenly, and stunningly, Stadler missed it.

The most general reaction was of incredulity, but a few of the crowd cheered and the Americans immediately assumed that they were cheering the miss, rather than the totally unexpected half that had fallen to the Europeans. They may, of course, have been quite right in their assumption and if that is so it is deeply regrettable, for there is no place in golf for that kind of behaviour. But it is difficult, if not impossible, to know just what a spectator's individual motivation is and the Americans were wrong to let it affect them as it evidently did. Indeed the American captain, Lee Trevino, berated his team some months later, saying: 'There are good losers and bad losers and my side got the socks beat off of them. I thought they were cry-babies and I told them that.'

It was the Europeans who came out fighting on the final day, none more so than Pinero who had wanted to take on Lanny Wadkins, allegedly the Americans' best in-fighter. He got him, at the top of the 12 singles, and he beat him. The word was passed down the line and The Belfry was ringing all day long to the sound of European cheers. Pinero's win made the match score 10–7, Stadler pulled one back for 10–8 and then Langer, Lyle and Paul Way made it 13–8. Ballesteros, three down to Tom Kite, got a half, and then Torrance, two down with four to play, beat the American champion North on the final green. Neither he nor, I suspect, a great many people in the crowd will ever have a more emotional moment.

Later in the year the Association of Golf Writers had to sit down and choose who was to hold their trophy for having done the most for European golf during 1985. There was not, of course, a choice at all and the whole Ryder Cup team was voted the worthiest recipients – which meant telling Bernhard Langer and Sandy Lyle that winning the Masters and the Open was not, this year anyway, enough!.

Langer had performed solidly indeed in Augusta, coming from two behind after three rounds to take the title. The leader that last day was Ray Floyd, a good front runner, followed by Curtis Strange who had had rounds of 80, 65

and 68 and, when asked if he had expected to be in such a position after his first round, admitted not only that he was 'surprised as hell' but also that he had not really expected to be playing golf at all, having made return flight reservations after his first round.

It almost seemed as though Strange was predestined to take the title but in the end the unconsidered Langer survived not only the pressure of the day but also of playing with Seve. The two had had their differences in the past, with Langer claiming that Ballesteros was an indifferent playing partner 'unless you keep telling him how good he is.' It was a rare example of open antagonism in golf and had been said at Wentworth where Langer was due to meet Ballesteros in the final of the World Match-Play Championship. But by Augusta the two men had become reconciled, and so, after losing in England, Langer was ready to win in America. He played the last 30 holes of the famous course in 10 under par and finished six under, the winner by two despite a bogey on the last hole.,

Like Langer, in any normal year Lyle would have collected all the awards and plaudits and, like Langer, would have deserved them. He became the first Briton since Tony Jacklin to win the Open, and he did so with a grit and determination rarely seen in this normally placid young man. Even before the Championship started he told me that if he was going to win an Open he felt it would be at Royal St George's or at Turnberry where length was such a crucial factor. That put extra pressure on him but, in turn, it was alleviated by his luck with the weather. Anyone playing in the morning of the first day and the afternoon of the second, as Lyle did, enjoyed reasonable July weather.

Anyone who had the reverse draw, as did half the field of course, got a mixture of rain, even occasional hail, and gale-force winds which made club selection impossible. Langer, a long hitter, was short of the short 16th (165 yd/151 m) with a well-hit four-iron. At the short 11th he was on the green, 220 yards (201 m) away with a seven-iron. His second-round 69 was probably the best of the Championship, but Lyle's 71 was not far behind and he and David Graham led on 139.

Lyle did not play well on Saturday, taking 73; a 'sloppy' round, he called it; so then he was three behind Langer and Graham, the new leaders for the final round.

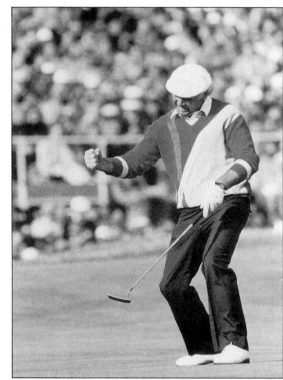

Christy O'Connor Jnr celebrates the sinking of another long putt at the 1985 Open.

Bernhard Langer, in contention up to the final green at Royal St George's in 1985.

There was, in a sense, an element of anticlimax to the 1985 Open. As in the Ryder Cup, it is always best when there is excitement or theatre at the finish and you could hardly have asked for more at The Belfry than for the winning putt to be a long one, to be a birdie and to be on the final green in front of the crowds. Lyle's winning putt was less than two feet, was for a bogey and was made all of 25 minutes before the men who could beat him even arrived on the last green. But drama there was in those closing holes, starting at the long 14th where Lyle, two behind the leaders, hooked into the rough and found an almost unplayable lie. He did well to get it out, short of the Suez Canal that crosses the fairway over 200 yards before the green. He then did extremely well to hit a one-iron onto the green and incredibly well to hole the 45-foot birdie putt.

That got him into the championship and it also, for once, made him respond positively. He fairly lashed his drive at the 15th, finishing 120 yards in front of playing partner Christy O'Connor Junior, and then hit his second to 12 feet. The putt went in and Lyle realized that the Open could be his with just a little steady play. Pars followed at the 16th and 17th, but not at the 18th. A good drive meant he needed a six-iron for his second shot, and as he and caddie Dave Musgrove consulted Lyle held out his hand for the club. 'Look at that,' he said, 'steady as a rock.'

He played a good shot, but it trickled into Duncan's Hollow, a nasty grassy dell on the left, and he debated for ages over what to do next. He elected to take a wedge and try to loft the ball up the sharp slope to the pin. 'I saw it as the correct shot,' he said afterwards, 'and I didn't want to just scuff it out anywhere on the green and take an easy five.' But the ball was just a fraction deeper in the grass than he thought, the connection was not good and his attempt, after nearly reaching the crest of the rise, ran back down again. Lyle, normally almost emotionless, sank to his knees and then buried his head in the grass.

The ball had stayed on the green, just, and now Lyle had an awful 25-footer, up the slope, and simply had to get down in only two more. It was then that he showed his class, with a magnificent putt that slid 18 inches past, and he holed, quickly, for a bogey. Then came a wait of around 25 minutes while two of the slowest players in the world, David Graham and

Bernhard Langer, played the last hole and a half, needing a birdie at either the 17th or 18th to tie with Lyle.

160

Sandy Lyle can't wait to get his hands on the Open trophy at the presentation ceremony in 1985.

Neither could get it, although Langer almost holed his final chip, and Sandy Lyle had fulfilled a talent that had long been evident. In doing so he had provided European golf with yet another high point, and he also proved, in passing, that nice guys can win.

Golf is played for the most part by nice people in nice places. It is unique in sport in that it is self-regulatory; if you transgress you call the penalty on yourself, and it is unique, too, in that if you fail to do so, and are caught, you may just as well give up the game there and then. In golf there is no playing to the umpire or referee. It is not an acceptable part of the game to get away with whatever you can, for if you did golf would simply cease to be worth playing.

Nothing could be easier, even during a closely observed round, than to move the ball a fraction and so turn an impossible shot into a possible one, or a difficult one into an easy one. The problem is that if you do there is no point in playing any more.

Therefore golf is played by honest people – or at the very least by people who are honest for the duration. It follows that there is no abusing of officials on the course, no ranting and raving *à la* McEnroe, and it is this aspect that not only appeals to vastly increasing numbers of the public, but also to the sponsors who are sick and tired of the Superbrats and their like believing themselves to be greater than the sport which created them. It has been said, and there is more than a grain of truth in it, that McEnroe has done more for golf than someone like Tom Watson in that he has driven sponsors into a cleaner and more acceptable sport.

There are many instances of how heinous a crime misbehaviour on the course is taken to be. In the qualifying round at Royal St George's in 1985, David Robertson, a Scot, was playing with an Englishman, Simon Middleham, and an American, Alvin Odom Junior. Neither they, nor his caddie who walked off after nine holes, could believe what they were seeing as Robertson set about trying to get into the Championship in a totally illegal manner. The caddie alleged that he moved the ball in the rough, the players alleged he moved the ball feet nearer the pin on the greens by pretending to put down a marker behind his ball (but not doing so in fact), so that he could replace the ball anywhere he felt like so doing.

After a couple of instances of this the R & A were called in, Robertson was disqualified and later the Professional Golfers' Association banned him from the game for 20 years. The Executive Director of the Tour, Ken Schofield, said 'This is a sad day for golf but the

decision was taken with a view to protecting the integrity of the game and as a warning to everybody.'

Nick Faldo comes into a much different category and his case is interesting in that he was reviled, probably wrongly at the actual time of the incident, for precisely the advantage-taking that goes on in other sports. He was playing Graham Marsh in the Suntory World Match-Play Championship at Wentworth when, at the 16th, he hit his second shot through the green. Faldo was having problems at the time, but the help he then got was both unwanted and illegal. Someone in the crowd threw the ball back onto the green and because no official, or either of the players, had seen it happen, the ball was allowed to stay there. Faldo, acting within the rules, went on to win a hole he had looked like losing, and the match.

He was criticized heavily at the time, and it is true to say that another player, having heard the facts, might have reacted differently. But Faldo was within his rights: where he went wrong was the next day. Then after seeing the countless replays of the incident on television, he refused to show any signs of contrition, to say something simple like 'I wouldn't have wanted to win like that.' Instead he insisted that he had behaved correctly, saying, 'I had to do what I did. This is the World Match-Play Championship, not the Wentworth Christmas Alliance.'

Thus he was perceived to have observed the rules, but not the spirit of the game, and the latter is so important that the Faldo-Marsh affair will probably never be forgotten. It was all a great pity. British sport is forever looking for white hopes and new heroes and Faldo, with a sporting concession the next day, would have gone a very long way towards being that in British golf.

If nothing else those incidents, and the rarity of them point up just why golf has the image it has and why, in an increasingly immoral world, the sport has boomed, and is so attractive to sponsors.

There is another potent reason for the boom. The Pro-Am is another aspect of golf that is all but unique in sport. No other major sport allows the veriest hacker to compete, at the same place and on level terms, with the game's superstars. Try batting against Michael Holding or playing squash against Jahangir Khan. Think of the impossibility of playing at Wembley or Wimbledon. But the Pro-Am allows you to play against Severiano Ballesteros or Greg Norman, at Muirfield or St Andrews, and the handicapping system means that you may be able to beat them. That is a powerful attraction to a sponsor, who knows that he, his friends or associates are likely to talk of nothing else once drawn to play in a Pro-Am with a really good player. The talk will, in fact, start as soon as the draw is known and go on for months afterwards, and the experience will be forever associated with the sponsor.

Top *No help from this spectator. Curtis Strange and Peter Jacobsen examine a difficult lie during the 1985 Ryder Cup at The Belfry.*

Above *Cricketer Ian Botham encourages his ball across the water and on to the green at the par-four 10th at The Belfry, watched by an enthusiastic Allan Border and fast-bowler Jeff Thomson, who seems to have exchanged his golf clubs for a can of XXXX.*

A Peugeot waits for anyone holing in one at La Moraleja during the 1986 Spanish Open.

Isao Aoki is presented with the keys to a flat worth £55,000 after his hole-in-one at Wentworth during the World Match-Play of 1979.

Big winnings for Miller Barber at the US Seniors' TPC in 1983.

I f all the periods of popularity and prosperity which golf has enjoyed in its long history, none compares with that of the last decade and, in particular, the last five years. The financial boom in that time has been quite extraordinary. A few simple figures illustrate the growth in purses on the two most important tours in the world, the American and the European. In 1979 the US Tour played for just under $13 million. Seven years later that had doubled and in 1987 the Americans played for $34 million. There is an official tournament in 46 of the 52 weeks of the year.

The story is similar, if on a smaller scale, in Europe. In 1979 the prize-money crossed the £1 million threshold. Since then it has grown substantially every year with the result that in 1987 the players toured Europe and Great Britain for £6½ million. There have been around 26 or 27 tournaments for each of the last five years, a number limited by the times and places it is possible to play golf in Europe because of the weather. But that figure is expected to expand. For three years Tunisia, in North Africa, was the starting point for the European Tour, and although the Tunisians dropped out in 1985, the Moroccan Open began in 1987 and it is in such areas that the PGA Tour is looking to extend its activities. There is talk of tournaments at both the beginning and end of the season in places such as Southern Spain and Sardinia.

Dramatic though the increases have been, the underlying worldwide trend is still upwards. Not only are there more tournaments for more money, but big-money events have proliferated too, and in 1987 America staged its first $2 million event, the Nabisco Grand Prix of Golf. The first prize was $360,000 and only the 30 leading players in the United States were eligible to compete for it.

Golf has also had its $½ million putt. The Mazda car company staged an event in Jamaica over a period of years for the top 12 players of the American Men's Senior Tour and the top 12 of the American Ladies' Tour. First prize, $250,000 each in the fourball format; second prize, $15,000 each.

The format means that every so often someone is faced with a putt which, if they hole it, wins prize-money of $500,000 to be shared between them. If they miss it they may end up with only $15,000 each. In successive years, 1985

A sizeable cheque for Amy Alcott after her win in the 1985 World Championship of Women's Golf.

and 1986, Lee Elder and Billy Casper both faced that particular putt; both missed it and had to settle for second place.

The first $1 million event was held in, of all places, Bophuthatswana and was called the Sun City Challenge. Only a handful of players were invited to compete and, as an invitation event, it had a curiosity value only. But the size of the prize broke new ground and it has rapidly been followed by events on the regular US Tour that also feature a prize fund of $1 million. In 1986 there were three of them and Greg Norman, who won one – the Panasonic Las Vegas Invitational – is convinced that the years leading into the 1990s will see that figure rise to a dozen or more.

It is not just the leading tours that are doing well. the US Ladies' Tour in 1979 was worth $4½ million, and has now grown to $11 million, while the US Seniors' Tour has taken off to an extent that few could ever have contemplated. In 1980 there were just two events, worth in total $250,000. Inside seven years they too were playing for $11 million.

In the course of all this not a few American professional golfers became dollar millionaires; on the two men's tours there were, by 1986, no fewer than 60 such still active. Some of them, like Jack Nicklaus, Tom Watson and Lee Trevino, made vast fortunes out of the game and Nicklaus has been called one of the 500 richest men in the United States. He has made over $4 million out of winnings alone; money he has used to set up businesses all over America. He is, for instance, involved in the building of dozens of golf courses at any one time and that, together with the property business that goes with the courses, means megabucks.

Trevino has won over $3 million but, in his happy-go-lucky way, managed to lose at least the first half of it through trusting too many people with too much of it.

Elsewhere in the world there is a flourishing Australasian circuit, a Safari Circuit in Africa, and in Japan and the Far East there are more tournaments than there are weeks to fit them into. As the interest grows, and leisure time increases, so too will purses around the world. The man or woman with a talent for golf is today a fortunate person.

Jack Nicklaus, undoubtedly the greatest over the last twenty years, with other great players of recent years.
Right *With Seve Ballesteros in 1982 during the Open Championship at Royal Troon.*
Below *With Greg Norman during the 1986 World Match-Play at Wentworth.*
Below right *With Lee Trevino at the Turnberry Open of 1977.*

One of the most extraordinary facets of golf is that it is such a difficult game that a player may only win two or three times a year and yet be recognized as one of the game's greats.

Jack Nicklaus, for example, is indisputably the greatest winner the game has ever known, and yet on his home ground – the US Tour – he averages only 2.84 wins per year. A tennis player who did likewise would be good, but certainly not great. Similarly the man who has dominated the American scene in the late Seventies and early Eighties, Tom Watson, averages only 1.94 wins per year. This is despite the fact that from 1977 to 1984 he led the American money list five times, he won five Opens, two US Masters Championships and one US Open. That is a stupendous record, but achieved on a striking rate that would leave a tennis player among the also-rans.

What emerges from these statistics is the enormous difficulty of the game. That, combined with the standards of excellence being achieved all round the world, means that it is consistency over a long period of time which is the true mark of a champion in golf. Nicklaus

has 71 wins over 25 years in America; Watson 31 in 16, and the next best, Lee Trevino, 27 in 20 for an average of 1.35.

Who, then, have been the great players since 1975? Nicklaus and Watson demonstrably,

Severiano Ballesteros certainly, and Greg Norman, while needing another Major or two and a few more years at the top, is seemingly certain to join them. On the European and US Tours Ballesteros emerges with an average of 3.15 wins per year over 13 years, while Norman, on the same basis, averages 2.57.

Ballesteros thus not only has the best average of any of the greats, he is also by far the most charismatic of them. Nicklaus is almost overpowering in his intensity, Watson strangely anonymous, and while Norman is an undoubted attraction it is the Spaniard who almost compels people to go and watch him.

Like Arnold Palmer before him, he has the ability to make things happen: to go into the trees, spot a two-foot gap, go for it and get it. Or not, as the case may be. The fact that his miracle recoveries come off more often than not; the fact that he will acknowledge the applause with a devastating smile from an all-too-handsome face; the fact that he will then often birdie the hole in question – all these have made him easily the biggest attraction in world golf since he won his first tournament, the Dutch Open, in 1976.

That came after he had burst upon the scene in the Open Championship of that year, at Royal Birkdale. Narrowly runner-up to Johnny Miller, he was only 19 and Miller said, probably correctly, at the presentation that it was as well Ballesteros had not won because it was a little too soon. 'But he'll win all right,' added Miller, and it took only three more years before the brothers Ballesteros – Severiano, Baldomero, Vicente and Manuel – were embracing one another, in tears, on the 18th green at Royal Lytham and St Annes.

The following year he destroyed the field in the US Masters and with nine holes to go he looked like destroying the Augusta course as well. He led by ten shots, but even as journalists were filling the early editions of the British papers with reports of Ballesteros 'shattering the cream of American professional golf' he began to drop shots, and at one stage his margin was down to two. However, at the 15th he hit one of the great four-iron shots of his life, birdied this intimidating par five and cruised home. It was ironic that six years later, faced with same shot and the same pressing need for a birdie, he dumped his ball into the water in front of the green and enabled Nicklaus to take a totally unexpected victory.

Niklaus with Isao Aoki at the US Open at Baltusrol in 1980, and (below) with Tom Watson during their epic struggle at Turnberry in the 1977 Open.

167

In Europe Ballesteros has an almost embarrassing superiority over the rest of the field. He has won a total of 11 times in 1985 and 1986 and it is a measure of the man that although he took home over £1 million in prize-money from all over the world, he counted those years unsatisfactory. He had not won a major championship in that time, his last being the 1984 Open at St Andrews.

He is a man with burning ambitions. He is aware of records, conscious of his place in the game and wants to establish beyond argument that he is one of the all-time great players. To do that he will need to win a US Open and perhaps a US PGA Championship, completing the modern Grand Slam, and no-one in world golf is more likely to do so.

Nicklaus, of course, has 'Slammed' three times, the third of them being completed when he won the US Open at Baltusrol in 1980. That he is the greatest champion in golf is disputed only by a few; that he is the longest-reigning champion is disputed by no-one. He won his first Major, the US Open, in 1962. His fourth, at Baltusrol, came 18 years later and featured a tremendous battle with Isao Aoki before Nicklaus gradually out-putted him. Nicklaus stayed in the Press Tent that evening

for nearly two hours, revelling in his triumph, and not a few people thought he might retire at that time. But not only did he continue, he went on to win the US PGA, for the fifth time, later in the year, his 17th major championship as a professional.

Surely now he would, at the age of 40, call it a day? But Nicklaus carried on – and on and on. By the time he had reached 46 only he can really have thought he was capable of another major championship win, and the thoughts of most were reflected in a newspaper article that Barbara, his wife, cut out and fixed on the door of the refrigerator at home before the 1986 Masters. 'Nicklaus is all washed up, it's time for a graceful retirement before he becomes a laughing stock' was the general theme, but by the end of the week Nicklaus had had, as is his wont, the last word.

He produced an amazing last nine holes of 30, coming from well behind to overtake the man who had dominated the Championship, Ballesteros. He was helped by the Spaniard's amazing mistake at the 15th, mentioned earlier, but also by his own incredible temperament. When the pressure came on he responded, as he always has, positively. Afterwards he said, almost plaintively: 'You know, I really don't

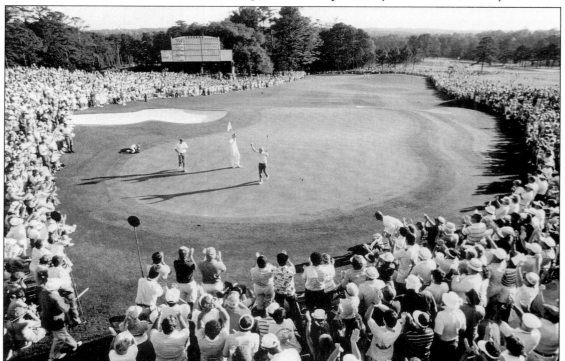

Jack Nicklaus wins yet another Major, this time the 1986 Masters.

understand putting. At a time when I really should not have been able to draw breath, let alone get the putter head back, I holed everything.'

Again the world's Press waited for the word 'retirement' and again it did not come. Nicklaus said he had decided not to play as much, but before anyone got the wrong idea, added: 'I feel that if I play well for a week I can still win a major championship.' The Golden Bear was still growling.

In the years 1971 to 1976 inclusive Nicklaus was first in the US money list five times and second once. It is a measure, then, of how good Tom Watson had to be to take over completely at the top from 1977 to 1980. Few people have ever played as aggressively as Watson, who went for the pin from almost anywhere, secure in the knowledge that he never missed from four feet. His reasoning was that if an aggressive shot came off he would have a four-foot birdie putt; if it did not he would, as one of the all-time wonders at chipping, get down in two from wherever he finished.

Strangely, despite this attractive philosophy, he never attracted the adulation of the American crowds who perhaps saw him as altogether too homespun, too modest a Huckleberry Finn figure. It is one of the ironies of sport that this great player is more popular in Great Britain, and particularly in Scotland where he has won four of his five Open Championships, than he is in his homeland.

It was at Pebble Beach, though, that he produced one of the single great shots of Championship golf. By 1982 Watson had won four British Open Championships and two Masters, but not his own Open. He came to the magnificent short 17th at Pebble Beach tied with Nicklaus who was already in the clubhouse – or, more accurately, in the scorer's tent by the 18th green waiting for the only man who could catch him.

Watson's tee shot was dragged left into heavy rough and it looked as if a three would be the absolute best he could do, a four much more likely. Instead, after telling his caddie he would do so, he holed for a birdie and set off on a triumphant run around the fringe of the green, confident that this shot had won him the title. He birdied the last hole as well and now needs only the US PGA title for a Grand Slam.

There is a flamboyance about Greg Norman, plus a highly developed sense of publicity and an equally well-proportioned amount of sportsmanship that makes him one of the most attractive golfers of the 1980s. The interplay between Norman and Fuzzy Zoeller in the 1984 US Open at Winged Foot, when first of all Zoeller 'surrendered' by waving a white towel at what he erroneously thought was a winning birdie putt by the Australian on the 72nd green, and then Norman's surrender of the title by waving a white handkerchief at the same spot when eight shots behind in an 18 hole play-off the next day, remains one of the great sporting actions of our age.

Great things have long been predicted for Norman, but they have been a relatively long time in coming. He won his first major championship – the Open – at Turnberry in 1986, when he was already 31. But it was, in every respect, an incredible year for Norman. No-one had ever led each of the four Majors after three rounds, as he did.

In the US Masters he, like Ballesteros, felt 'cheated' by Nicklaus's extraordinary charge through the field. In the US Open at Shinnecock Hills, he had a one-shot lead before, in his own words, 'coming out feeling flat' for the last round and losing to Ray Floyd. But Turnberry helped to make up for those. On a monstrously tight course and in generally vile weather he had a second round 63 which led, ultimately, to victory by five shots. Afterwards he was full of praise for Nicklaus who, he said, had passed on the advice that won him the Championship. 'Don't, under pressure, grip too tightly with the left hand,' said the man who should know. Typically, also, he went to the 18th green that night, at midnight, and celebrated by opening a few bottles of champagne.

It remained only for him to be robbed of the US PGA Championship. Bob Tway, after two superb and unlooked for recoveries at the the 15th and 17th for unlikely pars, holed his bunker shot at the 18th for a winning birdie when the best it seemed he could do would be to force a play-off.

Norman, happily, can shrug these things off. He went on to head the US money list with $653,296, a mere $516 ahead of Bob Tway. It is that priceless ability to ignore the inevitable hurt that Championship contests bring with them which makes it seem inevitable that Norman will go on to win more of them and take his place among the truly great players of the game.

The young Seve Ballesteros at the 1976 Open at Royal Birkdale and (far right) ten years later watching another young Spanish prodigy Jose Maria Olazabal during the European Open at Sunningdale.

Sandy Lyle in 1979, playing in the Ryder Cup at The Greenbrier.

In the mind's eye of many young, hopeful amateurs is a model golfing progression. Often it is like Sandy Lyle's:
Oct 1977 Turn professional and win qualifying school.
Feb 1978 Win first tournament entered as a pro, breaking the world 36-hole record en route with rounds of 61 and 63.
1979 Top the European money list.
1980 Top the European money list.
1985 Win Open Championship.
Or they may settle for the record of Jose Maria Olazabal:
Oct 1985 Turn professional and win qualifying school.
Sept 1986 Win Ebel European Masters at Crans-sur-Sierre.
Nov 1986 Finish second in European Order of Merit, beaten only by Severiano Ballesteros.

Timetables like those are fine in the imagination, but keeping to them in real life is another matter. For every Lyle and Olazabal there are dozens who fail or who carry on in sheer desperation, convinced that the odd good round is their normal game. The Royal and Ancient is deluged each year with applications to restore their amateur status from players who could not make enough to eat as a pro.

The bravest of the failures are those who admit it, who recognize their limitations and get out. Trevor Homer, for instance, won the British Amateur Championship in 1972 and 1974. He was a superb match-player, and on the strength of that turned professional. But almost no pro golf is match-play and in the two years that he gave himself to make the grade, he made almost nothing. Then, as he had said he would, he left the game, returned to his successful businesses in the Midlands and now hardly plays golf at all. Similarly, Martin Thompson won the British Amateur in 1982, but departed professional golf a couple of years later having spent a great deal more than he won.

Part of the problem, of course, is that the strugglers' hopes and ambitions are constantly being refuelled by the occasional and extraordinary success stories on golf tours around the world. Suddenly, from nowhere, a player who has given no indication that he would ever win a tournament, does so. The strugglers look at themselves, say that old so-and-so is certainly no better than they are, and decide to stay on the Tour for another

period of time. Massimo Mannelli, for instance, turned professional in 1968 and for the next 11 years barely did enough to stay on the Tour. Then he won the 1980 Italian Open. Similarly his countryman, Baldovino Dassu, hardly ever threatened the winners until, in 1976, he not only won the Dunlop Masters one week, he won the Italian Open the next. Neither player has, however, won on the European Tour since.

America, naturally, has even more extravagant stories. The first tournament of the 1987 season was held near San Diego, California and was won by Mac O'Grady. It was called the Tournament of Champions and, as its name implies, is open only to those who have won a tournament in the previous 12 months. In O'Grady's case that was the Greater Hartford Open, and it was his first victory as a professional, a status he had acquired 14 years previously. Not only that, though. He had attended the qualifying school in America no fewer than 17 times before getting his right to play the US Tour, a display of almost unparalleled belief in oneself. Even O'Grady, the man who said after his first victory that he 'wanted to go into the volcano and become as one with the lava' – even he was unable to

The persistent Mac O'Grady at the 1987 US Open.

Three of Britain's young hopefuls.
Right *Mark Roe.*
Below *Peter Baker.*
Facing page *Paul Curry.*

explain what kept him going for all those fruitless years. What he did say, though, was that after playing so many different places all round the world, scratching a living before getting his card, 'being on the US Tour is, for me, like celebrating Christmas every day.'

Things were almost as bad for Kenny Knox. He went to the school 11 times after turning professional in 1978 and by early 1986 he had such a low ranking in America that he was struggling to get into tournaments, let alone make any money. In order to get into the Honda event in Florida he had to take part in a pre-tournament qualifying event in which there were four tournament places available for 120 competitors. Knox got the fourth and so went into the 144-man field for the Honda as the 144th qualifier. He won the tournament and went on to win over $250,000 in 1986 and finished 24th in the American money list.

Both O'Grady and Knox appear to be set for life, within months of being almost destitute. In the light of their stories it is hardly surprising that the hopefuls continue to hope, and the strugglers continue to struggle on. As standards rise, however, it becomes more and more difficult for players to make a living, as

figures from the PGA European Tour School illustrate vividly. In 1980, 282 players tried for the card in Portugal and just over a quarter of them, 71, made it. Of that 71, 23 managed to earn enough money in 1981 to avoid having to go back to the school. Four years later 388 went through the school, in Spain, and only an eighth of them, i.e. 50, got through. Of that 50, only 19 survived the rigours of the Tour the next year.

The clichés come to life when applied to golf at this level. It was never meant to be fair; no–one said it was easy, but if you get the breaks it can be 'Christmas every day.'

s golf wanders the globe, it comes to rest in some unlikely places. There is a nine-hole little golf course to the north of Katmandu, for instance; the first $1 million tournament in the world was played in Bophuthatswana; there is a course built on an island composed of sand-dredgings in Singapore harbour, and I have to report that I am no better a player at Furnace Creek Golf Club, which is 200 feet or so below sea level in California's Death Valley, than I am at Crans-sur-Sierre 3,000 feet up a Swiss Alp.

Given such variety it is hardly surprising that for years professional golf has flourished in darkest Africa. The Safari Circuit, peopled principally by players from the PGA European Tour, plus a few local professionals, has had several useful functions. For the more successful professionals it serves as a fund-raiser and confidence booster for the sterner tests of the European season. For the local players it serves as a standard setter, letting them know how much there is still to achieve. Perhaps best of all, it acts as a banner for the game in places like

eagerness to display itself. The ex-pats in various African countries, starved of golf as played at its highest level, encouraged a few professionals to come out to give exhibitions and play a few holes. Principal among these was the late Dai Rees, the man who captained the winning 1957 Ryder Cup side against the Americans at Lindrick. There was no keener golfer in his lifetime than Dai. He always asked only that there should be a golf course, and people to beat – or people to beat into shape – and his life was complete. He loved playing, he loved teaching and in his boundless enthusiasm the Safari Tour was born.

It established itself and by the early 1980s it was worth around £350,000. Countless promising young players had used it to establish themselves. Principal among these was Sandy Lyle who won the Nigerian Open in 1978 and went on to become the best British player since Tony Jacklin.

The Safari Tour has its own special flavour. The players are billeted with local members – which often leads to enduring friendships but sometimes, with bath times and

An African-style green. This one is on the Griquatown golf course in South Africa. Because of the thick sand a player is allowed to place his ball on a hardened strip at a distance from the cup equal to that at which it finished on the approach shot.

Ikoyi, Nigeria; Nairobi, Kenya; Lusaka, Zambia and Yamoussoukrou in the Ivory Coast. There seems a good chance that Stanley's second question now to Dr Livingstone would be: 'Care for nine holes?'

The Safari Tour was born out of golf's

tee times to be considered, does not work out. The players play in colonial rig – shorts and long socks – and red-ant repellent and a red-nose resister are two essentials for the golf bag. Players also have to contend on occasions with the members' eagerness to be hospitable, which

beginning to show talent. John Ngugi, a Kikuyu from Kenya, led the Zambian Open at Lusaka after the first round in 1987 and was only a stroke behind after 36 holes.

In the Dunhill Cup the organizers, answering political expediency, have made a habit of inviting an African nation to play in their tournament even though, in the case of Zambia, they had only three professionals in total to make up the three-man team. But their experience of the Safari Tour helped them to cope with the rigours of St Andrews at the end of the year, and the same was true when Nigeria was the invited nation. Peter Akakasiaka found himself playing Severiano Ballesteros over the Old Course and, far from being overawed, grinned cheerfully for the photographers and only lost by a relatively small margin.

Nigeria and the Ivory Coast are two countries that have installed amazingly up-to-date golfing facilities. The Ikoyi Club in Lagos, for example, has 8,000 members and employs over 300 staff to service the golf course, two swimming pools, nine tennis, three badminton and seven squash courts as well as a five-star restaurant.

At Yamoussoukrou, four hours' drive from the Ivory Coast capital, Abidjan, a 27-hole lay-out has been created from nothing on the orders of the President, Félix Houphouet Boigny. There is also a hotel, an Olympic size pool, tennis, squash and a gymnasium.

Golf still owes something to presidential whim in Africa, and despite all the troubles in the South the game in the front-line state of Zambia has always been encouraged by the Head of State, Kenneth Kaunda. A keen and effective 16 handicap player, he organized every year a match between his own State House team and the professionals who were in the country for the Zambia Open. It was played on the nine-hole course laid out in the grounds of State House and the home team currently lead the series comfortably. The President denies that his team only declare their handicaps after the match is over!

That kind of occasion is part of the reason for the success of the Safari Tour which has raised the flag in some unexpected quarters and made friendships that could have been made no other way. All those men who worked with Dai Rees to start it all have reason to be both pleased and proud of themselves.

Peter Akakasiaka playing in the 1985 Dunhill Cup against Seve Ballesteros.

Zambian President Kenneth Kaunda partners Brian Barnes in the Pro-Am before the 1982 Zambian Open.

can lead to a few desperate dashes to get to the 1st tee on time, but altogether the Safari Tour was, and is, a marvellous training ground, both on and off the course, for the young Europeans.

It has been useful, too, for the indigenous players, some of whom are

The names of Hicks, Seignious and Griffin may not rank alongside the Big Three of Player, Palmer and Nicklaus in the public imagination but they deserve their place in golfing history.

In 1944 they founded the Women's Professional Golf Association in the United States and though by 1948 it had, in the words of Betty Hicks, 'just sort of faded away,' it provided the starting point for the Ladies' Professional Golf Association which is blossoming as never before. In 1987 the LPGA was offering its members prize-money totalling nearly $11 million – an increase of 21,000 per cent since the days of Babe Zaharias, Betsy Rawls and Louise Suggs in the early 1950s.

In 1975 the LPGA's prize-money had moved over the million dollar mark but the whole organization was hovering on the verge of bankruptcy until a dynamic young marketing man called Ray Volpe became the Association's first commissioner and set about selling the tour with rare skill and enthusiasm.

Volpe had several outstanding players at his disposal – people such as Kathy Whitworth, Sandra Haynie and JoAnne Carner – but what

every sport needs in order to fulfil its potential is a player at the top who is not only demonstrably the best but who is also attractive, charming, full of joie de vivre and, preferably, highly photogenic. In short, someone who wins the hearts and minds of the public.

Women's golf in America acquired such a person in 1977 when Nancy Lopez turned professional. With her ready smile and outgoing demeanour her appeal was obvious. And she could play golf. And how. In her first full season, 1978, at the age of 21, she broke virtually every record in the LPGA book – most money won ($189,813); best stroke average (71.76); and – the most valuable achievement in terms of publicity – most victories in a row (five).

Nancy won nine tournaments in all that season and had the unique distinction of being both Rookie of the Year and Player of the Year, but it was those five wins in succession that excited everybody and pushed women's golf into a position of unusual prominence on the sports pages. The great Mickey Wright and Kathy Whitworth had both won four times in a row and everyone wanted to see if this not-so-raw rookie could make it five. Camera crews, photographers, reporters and fans descended on

Laura Baugh and (far right) Jan Stephenson, two glamorous competitors who helped attract large crowds to the US LPGA Tour in the 70s.

Nancy Lopez and caddy at the World Championship of Women's Golf in 1985.

JoAnne Carner encourages a long putt during the Colgate European Women's Championship at Sunningdale in 1975.
Facing page Laura Davies seems concerned about the outcome of her shot during the Ladies' Open at Royal Birkdale in 1986, which she went on to win.

Rochester, New York, for what was an aptly named tournament, in view of the way Nancy was raking in the cheques. It was the Bankers Trust Classic and, of course, Nancy won.

She came from behind to do it and admitted she had felt the pressure for the first time, explaining: 'I'm very competitive and I really wanted to be the only one ever to win five in a row.'

Her confidence and her putting saw her through and what really impressed JoAnne Carner – herself one of the all-time greats – was Nancy's composure: 'She handled the pressure unbelievably. In fact she seemed to thrive on it. For someone that young not to be overwhelmed was the most amazing thing.'

Nancy proved it was not just beginner's luck by winning eight tournaments the following year and finishing number one again. In each of the next four years she won at least twice, as well as fitting in marriage, divorce, marriage again – to baseball star Ray Knight – and the birth of her first child.

Beth Daniel – a teammate of Nancy when the United States won the Curtis Cup at Lytham in 1976 – usurped her as top professional in 1980 and 1981, with Carner taking over in 1982 and 1983 and Betsy King hitting the top spot the following year. Back came Lopez in 1985, winning five times and becoming the first LPGA player to earn over $400,000 in a year. She was Player of the Year for the third time and won her third Vare Trophy – awarded to the player with the best stroke average. She was only one win away from a coveted place in the Hall of Fame, so what did she do? She took most of 1986 off to have her second baby.

Pat Bradley, for ten years the most consistent player on the Tour and twice runner-up to Lopez as Player of the Year, at last made number one. Nobody deserved it more. She won nearly $½ million, a record for any one year, and of her five victories, three were in major championships. The Grand Slam eluded her when she finished fifth in the US Open but she had the satisfaction of becoming the first player to earn more than $2 million on the LPGA Tour. Carner joined her later in the season.

It is impossible to keep Lopez out of the limelight, though. In February 1987, just a month after her 30th birthday, she won for the 35th time on the Tour to become only the 11th member of the Hall of Fame, joining the likes of

Vivien Saunders, a driving force in British women's golf both on and off the course.

Zaharias, Wright, Whitworth and Carner.

There are a lot of very good players on the LPGA Tour. Two or three have won more money than Lopez; a few have won more tournaments; many have won more US Open Championships – she has yet to win one. But there remains the feeling that if everyone played her best, Nancy would come out on top. And there remains the certainty that, win or lose, none would be more charismatic.

She is the one name that can be guaranteed to sell tickets to a tournament, to get the attention of every sports editor within miles of an event. She is the most valuable asset that her branch of golf has ever possessed. And, at last, in that respect at least, she has a European counterpart.

Laura Davies has been taking the WPGA Tour – modern, non-American version – by storm. She turned professional in 1985 at the age of 21 and surprised everyone, including herself, by topping the money list with winnings of £21,736. She did it again in 1986, earning considerably more – £37,500 – as the Tour's stock rose, particularly on the Continent. For most of the season it had looked as though Liselotte Neumann of Sweden would become the first non-Briton to head the money list but Laura pipped her by winning two of the last three tournaments, the Ladies' British Open at Royal Birkdale and the La Manga Club Spanish Ladies' Open, the last event of the season.

Laura is tall, blonde and punches her weight. To put it unscientifically, she hits the ball miles. There is a buzz in the crowd when she steps onto the tee and, usually, awed gasps when she sends her drive soaring 260 yards or more down the middle. She is just what the WPGA needs after years of struggling to persuade people that women professionals were worth watching.

Eight years after the Tour got off the ground in 1979, it was worth over £1 million and people like Vivien Saunders – a founder of the Association and a tireless campaigner for the cause of women's professional golf – must have been heartened to note that the best amateurs were beginning to see the Tour as the next step in their development, rather than as a no-go area peopled by the brave and the bad.

A few months after helping Great Britain and Ireland to their historic victory in the Curtis Cup at Prairie Dunes in Kansas – they were the first side, male or female, amateur or

professional, to beat the Americans on their home soil – Patricia Johnson and Lillian Behan turned professional, something distinguished veteran teammates like Belle Robertson and Mary McKenna had never considered doing. America was really the only place for them to

Belle Robertson and Mary McKenna, a powerful combination.

make a living as a professional and neither of them was attracted by the life. They saw Vivien Saunders struggling valiantly there after taking the bold decision to turn professional in 1969 and were not inclined to follow her.

Now, golf in Europe is on the upswing with the Continent eager to stage at least half of the WPGA's events in some style, while Britain, traditionally more wary of females on the links, becomes aware that arranging the flowers on Captain's Day may not be the highlight of a girl's golfing career.

In April 1982 Peter Thomson, semi–retired from professional golf, failed to get elected to the Australian Parliament by a mere 4 per cent of the vote. Thomson – 'I've been interested in politics since I was 20' – decided that as it might be some time before the next election he would, in the interim, take a look at the burgeoning US Seniors' Tour, and in so doing started one of the most remarkable episodes that sport has ever known.

The Seniors, which began life in 1980 with two events and $250,000 in total prize money had, by the time of Thomson's decision, risen to 11 tournament and $1,400,000. Since then it has become a full Tour of 35 events with $9 million on offer. One of the substantial reasons for that dramatic rise has been the part played in it by people like Thomson. The Seniors has built itself on a keen appreciation of the realities of life and if there is one thing that players like Thomson, and Chi Chi Rodriguez, Arnold Palmer, Don January, Gary Player and Gay Brewer know all about it is how to keep the sponsors and punters happy.

The Pro–Ams that precede each Seniors' Tour event have become legendary for their goodwill and bonhomie, a contrast with the all–too–often dour occasion that goes before a regular tournament. As a consequence the growth of the Tour has been astounding and some of the participants have won more money in their Senior years than they did in the whole of their previous career.

One outstanding example is the 1963 Open Champion Bob Charles who, in a long and successful career, mostly in Europe but also in America and Australasia still did not win as much in over 20 years as he did in the first nine months of his time on the Senior Tour. In tournament play Charles won $261,000 and then, in December 1986, he went to Jamaica to play in the Mazda Champions event. That carries with it a first prize of $250,000 for each partner in a four-ball event and the New Zealander, in partnership with Amy Alcott, won. The $511,160 he won in 1986 was more than double his lifetime earnings in Europe, a profitable form of pension indeed.

In many ways the story of Peter Thomson is even more dramatic. For a couple of years he only pottered about on the Tour, then in 1984 he began to give it his full attention. In September of that year he won the World Seniors' Invitational and by September of the following year he had won a further nine tournaments. He totally dominated the Tour, giving it, as a five times British Open Champion, both status and impetus, as well as exciting a determination by the home professionals to remove him from the number one position. There has never been much love lost between Thomson and the American golfing profession, largely because he felt they never accorded his achievements in the Open sufficient respect. Now he was in America,

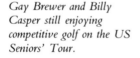

Gay Brewer and Billy Casper still enjoying competitive golf on the US Seniors' Tour.

beating all the men who had damned him with faint praise two decades earlier. It was a totally satsisfactory year for Thomson and it also helped to place the Tour in the public eye.

As the Tour has grown it has acquired more and more players who have passed the eligible age, 50, and it is becoming harder and harder to win. For instance, Gary Player became elegible in late 1985 and won his first tournament. But in 1986, although he won three times, he was beaten into fifth place in the money list, which was won by Bruce Crampton who took away over $450,000 – a sum, incidentally, which would have earned him sixth place on the regular Tour. Crampton won seven times, Don January and Dale Douglass four times each.

They are not exactly giving the money away, though. Bob Charles had 22 rounds successively of par or less and still did not win a tournament, while Miller Barber, the second most successful Senior of all time with $1,200,000 after the 1986 season, established a record of four successive 66s, six under par each time, in winning the Suntree Classic in 1982. The only other millionaire up to that point was Don January, with $200,000 more than Barber, but nothing seems more certain than that these ageing, but not fading, legends of the game will go on to provide years more entertainment yet. After all, in the 1986 money list the top 20 were all over the $100,000 prize-money mark, and there can be little greater incentive than that.

The flamboyant Chi-Chi Rodriguez, always a popular figure.

Don January, another Senior, enjoying a prolonged golfing career.

183

The tented village before the 1984 Open at St Andrews.

For Joe Flanagan, organizer for a quarter of a century of the Carrolls Irish Open, one of Europe's most successful tournaments, it is the crack, the fun, that counts. Golf is only a game after all.

But that is a relaxed, Irish view of things, not necessarily typical. It is not all fun setting up a tournament. Gone are the days when you put up a table at the 1st tee, handed out the cards to the players and collected them when they came back in. Modern professional golf is a multi-million pound business, it is the circus coming to town and hundreds of people are needed to make it work.

Tournament organizers are the ringmasters. They co-ordinate the whole show, liaising with the PGA European Tour people, the host club, the sponsors, and so on and on and on. Catering, car parking, ticket sales, publicity, security, courtesy cars, tentage, plumbers, electricians, sign writers, the printing of programmes...all these things and more have to be taken into account. One promoter has a briefing document of 78 pages, detailing what has to be done each day, and his own private planning document runs to 140 pages.

The European Tour's blueprint is a more modest 19 pages but seems to cover everything from play-off arrangements, the amount of sand in the bunkers and the number of telephones in the Press tent to traffic control, the dismantling of grandstands and the collection of caddies' bibs.

The well-equipped golf photographer: Phil Sheldon (centre) with all the necessary hardware and additional support from helpers Tim Henley (left) and Jan Traylen (right).

Meetings with the club, the local police and the St John Ambulance Brigade take place months before the event is staged to check on-course preparation, car parking facilities, traffic organization, signposting and a host of other details. Two or three weeks before the tournament metal roads are laid down, scaffolding put up and the course resounds with the squealing of drills, the thudding of hammers and the dull muttering of inconvenienced members.

Accommodating a tournament means disruption on a large scale, even for clubs that are so used to hosting big events that all they need to do is change the date and name of the event at the top of their tried and tested dossier. Not only are the clubhouse and course taken over but a tented village springs up, complete with hospitality tents, hamburger stalls and all the catering paraphernalia that goes with them,

A TV boom hovers over the Swilcan Burn at the 1984 Open.

as well as various stalls selling anything from clubs to furry headcovers, enamelled coins to toffee.

Should the tournament be televised, that is another hundred or more people to be taken into account, plus a couple of pantechnicons, numerous smaller vehicles and 30 miles of cable. Everybody prays for dry weather, not least because the heavy vehicles needed to transport goods and equipment do not operate well in a self-churned sea of mud. Neither are engineers, caterers, spectators or players at their best with rain trickling down their neck.

The tournament organizer cannot control the weather but he is responsible for everything else. Corporal Jones's *Dad's Army* motto of 'Don't panic, don't panic' seems to be the key, along with a keen eye for damage limitation. At one event, mysterious flooding in part of the tented village mystified and inconvenienced everybody until it was discovered that a dead bog was blocking the drainage system. It was up to the tournament organizer to have it removed.

At another event access to the car parks was limited and the build-up of traffic was causing chaos, not to mention fraying tempers. It was the tournament organizer's decision to speed up the process by letting the cars in free.

A cool head, a small, well-briefed team of right-hand men or women and a walkie-talkie in full working order are vital parts of the tournament organizer's equipment if he is to be successful at co-ordinating what one of the breed describes as the 'hives of craziness' that make up a golf tournament.

It is chastening to think that the great army of greenkeepers, chefs, Rules officials, secretaries, marshalls, car park attendants, journalists, photographers, courtesy car drivers, scorers and gladhanders that scurry around at a tournament from dawn to dusk are there because a few persons are playing a few rounds of golf for a large sum of money.

Money, now there is the word. That is why this great travelling circus cavorts its way round Europe for several months of the year, from El Prat to Wentworth, from Crans-sur-Sierre to Gleneagles. It makes money for the players, the PGA, the promoters, the caterers

Golf professional Tony Charnley and his wife Lucienne arrive for another tournament.

(excepting, perhaps the sad-faced purveyors of ice cream braving a British summer), for charities, and, ultimately, the sponsors.

Sponsors like golf. It has an honest image; it is often played in congenial surroundings; its top practitioners are not given to arguing with the referee or making rude gestures to the crowd; its less-exalted practitioners are ever ready to spend money on the latest gimmick and if they cannot play like Seve, they are more than willing to wear his watch, use his petrol or eat his breakfast cereal.

Golf tournaments last all day for four days (five if you include the pro-am), so sponsors have ample opportunity to entertain clients, business associates and people in high places. If you have Seve, Greg or Bernhard in your tournament, you will not have much trouble persuading people to come and watch, whether at your expense or their own.

And if the man in charge has got it right, if the fairway ropes are in the right place, the daily pairing sheets clearly printed, the hamburgers cooked and the loos unblocked, you may even, like Joe Flanagan, get singing in the public bar at the close of play.

Alex Harvey, the R & A's engraver, once again adds the name of Severiano Ballesteros to the Open Trophy before the 1984 presentation.

ACKNOWLEDGEMENTS

The Publishers would like to thank the following sources for their help in providing illustrations. (Where there is more than one illustration on a page, the credits start with the picture furthest to the left and nearest to the top and work down each column.)

Allied National Brands 163*b*

Associated Press 89, 95*b*, 124*b*

BBC Hulton Picture Library 10, 11*a* & *b*, 18, 34, 46*a* & *b*, 48*a* & *b*, 49*a*, 50, 51*a*, 52*a* & *b*,53*a* & *b*, 57*a* & *b*, 58*c*, 59*a*, *b* & *c*, 62, 64*b*, *c* & *d*, 68*b* & *c*, 70*a* & *b* & *c*, 72, *b c*, 73*a*, *b*, *c* & *d*. 74, 76

S.H. Benson 124*a*

Peter Dazeley 145*a*, 187*b*

Hailey Sports Photographics 157*c*

The Illustrated London News 17, 21, 24*b*, *c* & *d*, 26*b*, 28*a*, *b* & *c*, 30*b*, 31*b*, 32*a*, 33*a*, *b* & *c*, 35, 36*a*, *b* & *c*, 39*a*, 40*a*, 54*c*, 61

National Museum of Antiquities, Edinburgh 39*a*

The Bert Neale Collection 82*a*, 85*a*, *b* & *c*, 86*a* & *b*, 87*a* & *b*, 88, 96*b* & *c*, 97*a*, & *b*, 98*b*, 99, 100*a*, & *b*, 101*a* & *b*, 106, 107*a* & *b*, 117, 118b, 119, 120*b*, 121*a* & *b*, 122, 123, 126, 127*a* & *c*, 128, 129*a*, 131*a*, 133, 136, 137, 138*a*, 141*a*, & *b*, 143*a*, 149*b*, 153*b*, 178b

New York Times Photos 69*b*

Planet News 81

The Photosource 51*b*, 54*b*, 58b, 70*c*, 71, 84*a* & *b*, 90*a*, *b* & *c*, 91*b*, 93*a*, & *b*, 94*a*, 95*b*, 96*a*, 98*a*, 102*a*, & *b*, 103*a* & *b*, 104*a* & *b*, 105, 109, 110, 118*a*, 127*b*, 129*b*, 130*a* & *b*, 131*b*, 134, 135, 138*b*, 139, 140, 148*b*, 149*a*, 153*a*, 154, 174, 176, 177

Press Association 125, 127*b*

Phil Sheldon 16*b*, 27*b*, 42*a*, *b* & *c*, 43*a*, *b* & *c*, 58*a*, 83, 114*a*, *b* & *c*, 115*a*, *b* & *c*, 149*a*, *b*, *c*, *d* & *e*, 150*a*, *b* , *c*, *d* & *e*, 151*a*, *b*, *c* & *d*,152*a*, *b*, *c*, *d*, *e* & *f*, 156*a*, *b* & *c*, 157*a*, 158*a*, & *b*, 159*a* & *b*, 161, 162*a* & *b*, 163*a* & *c*, 164*a*, *b* & *c*, 165, 166*a*, *b* & *c*, 167*a* & *b*, 168, 170*a* & *b*, 171*a* & *b*, 172*a* & *b*, 173, 174*b*, 175*a*, 178*a*, 179, 180, 181, 182, 183*a* & *b*, 184*a* & *b*, 185, 186, 187*a*, & *c*

Sport and General 142*a*, 144*a*

Sportslines 157*b*

Sports Photographics 145*b*

Topical Press 23, 64*a*, 65*a* & *b*, 66*b*

UPI 82*b*, 120*a*

United States Golf Association 24*a*, 25

The Publishers are also grateful to Golf Illustrated for allowing access to their archives and to Sarah Baddiel of The Book Gallery, Gray's Antique Market, London W1 for making available for photography many items of golfiana.

GOLF · A WAY OF LIFE   GOLF · A WAY OF LIFE   GOLF · A WAY OF LIFE   GOLF · A WAY OF LIFE
GOLF · A WAY OF LIFE   GOLF · A WAY OF LIFE   GOLF · A WAY OF LIFE   GOLF · A WAY OF LIFE
GOLF · A WAY OF LIFE   GOLF · A WAY OF LIFE   GOLF · A WAY OF LIFE   GOLF · A WAY OF LIFE
GOLF · A WAY OF LIFE   GOLF · A WAY OF LIFE   GOLF · A WAY OF LIFE   GOLF · A WAY OF LIFE
GOLF · A WAY OF LIFE   GOLF · A WAY OF LIFE   GOLF · A WAY OF LIFE   GOLF · A WAY OF LIFE
GOLF · A WAY OF LIFE   GOLF · A WAY OF LIFE   GOLF · A WAY OF LIFE   GOLF · A WAY OF LIFE
GOLF · A WAY OF LIFE   GOLF · A WAY OF LIFE   GOLF · A WAY OF LIFE   GOLF · A WAY OF LIFE
GOLF · A WAY OF LIFE   GOLF · A WAY OF LIFE   GOLF · A WAY OF LIFE   GOLF · A WAY OF LIFE
GOLF · A WAY OF LIFE   GOLF · A WAY OF LIFE   GOLF · A WAY OF LIFE   GOLF · A WAY OF LIFE
GOLF · A WAY OF LIFE   GOLF · A WAY OF LIFE   GOLF · A WAY OF LIFE   GOLF · A WAY OF LIFE
GOLF · A WAY OF LIFE   GOLF · A WAY OF LIFE   GOLF · A WAY OF LIFE   GOLF · A WAY OF LIFE
GOLF · A WAY OF LIFE   GOLF · A WAY OF LIFE   GOLF · A WAY OF LIFE   GOLF · A WAY OF LIFE
GOLF · A WAY OF LIFE   GOLF · A WAY OF LIFE   GOLF · A WAY OF LIFE   GOLF · A WAY OF LIFE
GOLF · A WAY OF LIFE   GOLF · A WAY OF LIFE   GOLF · A WAY OF LIFE   GOLF · A WAY OF LIFE
GOLF · A WAY OF LIFE   GOLF · A WAY OF LIFE   GOLF · A WAY OF LIFE   GOLF · A WAY OF LIFE
GOLF · A WAY OF LIFE   GOLF · A WAY OF LIFE   GOLF · A WAY OF LIFE   GOLF · A WAY OF LIFE
GOLF · A WAY OF LIFE   GOLF · A WAY OF LIFE   GOLF · A WAY OF LIFE   GOLF · A WAY OF LIFE
GOLF · A WAY OF LIFE   GOLF · A WAY OF LIFE   GOLF · A WAY OF LIFE   GOLF · A WAY OF LIFE
GOLF · A WAY OF LIFE   GOLF · A WAY OF LIFE   GOLF · A WAY OF LIFE   GOLF · A WAY OF LIFE
GOLF · A WAY OF LIFE   GOLF · A WAY OF LIFE   GOLF · A WAY OF LIFE   GOLF · A WAY OF LIFE
GOLF · A WAY OF LIFE   GOLF · A WAY OF LIFE   GOLF · A WAY OF LIFE   GOLF · A WAY OF LIFE
GOLF · A WAY OF LIFE   GOLF · A WAY OF LIFE   GOLF · A WAY OF LIFE   GOLF · A WAY OF LIFE
GOLF · A WAY OF LIFE   GOLF · A WAY OF LIFE   GOLF · A WAY OF LIFE   GOLF · A WAY OF LIFE
GOLF · A WAY OF LIFE   GOLF · A WAY OF LIFE   GOLF · A WAY OF LIFE   GOLF · A WAY OF LIFE
GOLF · A WAY OF LIFE   GOLF · A WAY OF LIFE   GOLF · A WAY OF LIFE   GOLF · A WAY OF LIFE
GOLF · A WAY OF LIFE   GOLF · A WAY OF LIFE   GOLF · A WAY OF LIFE   GOLF · A WAY OF LIFE
GOLF · A WAY OF LIFE   GOLF · A WAY OF LIFE   GOLF · A WAY OF LIFE   GOLF · A WAY OF LIFE
GOLF · A WAY OF LIFE   GOLF · A WAY OF LIFE   GOLF · A WAY OF LIFE   GOLF · A WAY OF LIFE
GOLF · A WAY OF LIFE   GOLF · A WAY OF LIFE   GOLF · A WAY OF LIFE   GOLF · A WAY OF LIFE
GOLF · A WAY OF LIFE   GOLF · A WAY OF LIFE   GOLF · A WAY OF LIFE   GOLF · A WAY OF LIFE
GOLF · A WAY OF LIFE   GOLF · A WAY OF LIFE   GOLF · A WAY OF LIFE   GOLF · A WAY OF LIFE
GOLF · A WAY OF LIFE   GOLF · A WAY OF LIFE   GOLF · A WAY OF LIFE   GOLF · A WAY OF LIFE
GOLF · A WAY OF LIFE   GOLF · A WAY OF LIFE   GOLF · A WAY OF LIFE   GOLF · A WAY OF LIFE
GOLF · A WAY OF LIFE   GOLF · A WAY OF LIFE   GOLF · A WAY OF LIFE   GOLF · A WAY OF LIFE
GOLF · A WAY OF LIFE   GOLF · A WAY OF LIFE   GOLF · A WAY OF LIFE   GOLF · A WAY OF LIFE
GOLF · A WAY OF LIFE   GOLF · A WAY OF LIFE   GOLF · A WAY OF LIFE   GOLF · A WAY OF LIFE
GOLF · A WAY OF LIFE   GOLF · A WAY OF LIFE   GOLF · A WAY OF LIFE   GOLF · A WAY OF LIFE